THE POWER OF
PRAYERFUL

FASTING

&

PRAYER

**Fasting with Purpose and A Christian
Guide to Transformative Prayer**

Soulful Grace

The Power of Prayerful Fasting and Prayer:
Fasting with Purpose and A Christian Guide to Transformative Prayer

Copyright © 2023
Christ Glory Interpreters

ISBN:
9798873470426

Imprint:
Independently published

Acknowledgment

I give thanks from the bottom of my heart to the Almighty, the source of all power and knowledge, for guiding me while I was writing this work. I have had your heavenly inspiration as a constant companion, illuminating my path as I have entered the domain of spiritual combat.

I would especially like to thank my family, whose understanding and constant support made my quest possible. My commitment to this undertaking was fueled by your encouragement. I would want to express my gratitude to my friends for their understanding, support, and rare times of relaxation that helped me stay motivated.

My sincere gratitude goes out to the spiritual leaders and mentors who have contributed their knowledge and understanding, adding significant insights to this book. I am appreciative of your influence on my spiritual path; your counsel has been priceless.

I hope that anybody who uses this fasting and prayer guide will find liberation and transformation on their path. Your readiness to go into the depths of spiritual battle is admirable and motivational.

Finally, I would like to express my gratitude to all of the many people who helped shape "The Power of Prayerful Fasting and Prayer" whether directly or indirectly. Your combined energy and prayers have given this guide a resonance that goes beyond its written words.

I trust that the impact of this work will serve as a witness to the strength that comes from praying together, the steady light that leads us through life's invisible struggles, and the power of prayer.

How to Navigate This Prayer Guide

Welcome to "The Power of Prayerful Fasting and Prayer: Fasting with Purpose and A Christian Guide to Transformative Prayer." Enhance your spiritual journey with these steps:

1. Set Your Intention:

   Clarify your spiritual goals and intentions. Use the introduction space to articulate your purpose, be it seeking divine guidance, deepening your connection with God, or personal transformation.

2. Understand the Structure:

   Familiarize yourself with the organized sections. Each part builds on the previous, providing a progressive experience in fasting and prayer.

3. Daily Reflections:

   Engage with daily reflections and questions. Use a journal to record thoughts and insights, fostering self-discovery during your journey.

4. Practical Tips:

   Discover practical insights for integrating fasting and prayer into daily life. These tips guide you in creating a sustainable practice that aligns with your lifestyle.

5. Personalize Your Experience:

    Tailor practices to suit your unique needs. Modify fasting methods, prayer prompts, and reflections to resonate with your personal journey.

6. Community Engagement:

    Consider joining a community or study group for shared experiences. Discussion questions at the end of each chapter facilitate group conversations.

7. Rituals and Routines:

    Integrate suggested rituals into daily life. Establish a prayer space, adopt a fasting schedule, or incorporate mindful practices to support spiritual growth.

8. Celebrate Milestones:

    Acknowledge and celebrate achievements. Express gratitude for completing a fast, achieving a breakthrough in prayer, or experiencing transformative moments along the journey.

Contents

Introduction

Unveiling the Sacred Journey

I n the tapestry of our spiritual existence, there exists a sacred path—one paved with the stones of prayer and adorned with the blossoms of fasting. "The Power of Prayerful Fasting and Prayer: Fasting with Purpose and A Christian Guide to Transformative Prayer" is an invitation to partake in this divinely guided exploration, opening our hearts to the profound truths woven into the fabric of God's Word.

> Commit to the Lord whatever you do, and he will establish your plans.
>
> Proverbs 16:3 (NIV)

In the hustle of our modern lives, where time slips through our fingers like sand, the call to prayerful fasting echoes with a timeless urgency. This book is more than a guide; it is a journey fueled by purpose, sustained by faith, and illuminated by the transformative power of prayer.

> Is not this the kind of fasting I have chosen: to loose the chains of injustice and untie the cords of the yoke, to set the oppressed free and break every yoke?: Is it not to share your food with the hungry and to provide the poor wanderer with shelter—when you see the naked, to clothe them, and not to turn away from your

own flesh and blood?: Then your light will break forth like the dawn, and your healing will quickly appear; then your righteousness will go before you, and the glory of the Lord will be your rear guard: Then you will call, and the Lord will answer; you will cry for help, and he will say: Here am I. "If you do away with the yoke of oppression, with the pointing finger and malicious talk.

Isaiah 58:6-9 (NIV)

This verse reminds us of the chosen nature of fasting, not as a mere ritual but as a channel through which our spirits commune with the Divine. As we navigate the realms of purposeful fasting, guided by biblical wisdom, we are reminded of the transformative potential inherent in seeking God's presence.

Come near to God and he will come near to you. Wash your hands, you sinners, and purify your hearts, you double-minded.

James 4:8 (NIV)

This verse beckons us to draw near to God, promising that He, in turn, will draw near to us. Within these pages, discover the power of intentionality—setting forth with a clear purpose grounded in the Word of God. Fasting with purpose is an act of devotion, a deliberate turning towards the divine, seeking alignment with the Creator's plan for our lives.

Do not be anxious about anything, but in every situation, by prayer and petition, with thanksgiving, present your requests to God: And the peace of God, which transcends all understanding, will guard your hearts and your minds in Christ Jesus.

Philippians 4:6-7 (NIV)

This verse also encourages us not to be anxious but to present our requests to God through prayer, with thanksgiving, promising a peace that transcends understanding. As we delve into the heart of prayer, remember that each whispered petition is a conversation with the Almighty. Our prayers, like fragrant incense, ascend to the heavens, creating a sacred dialogue that transcends the boundaries of the earthly realm.

The chapters that follow will guide you through the rhythmic dance of fasting and prayer, offering practical insights, biblical reflections, and moments of profound revelation. Together, let us walk in the footsteps of the faithful who, throughout the ages, have found solace, strength, and transformation in the sacred discipline of prayerful fasting.

Your word is a lamp for my feet, a light on my path.

Psalm 119:105 (NIV)

Psalm 119:105 (NIV) assures us As you turn the pages of this book, may the light of God's Word illuminate your path, revealing the transformative power that awaits those who embark on the sacred journey of prayerful fasting. May your heart be open, your spirit receptive, and may the presence of the Holy Spirit guide you every step of the way.

The sacred discipline of fasting and prayer is not a distant ritual but a living expression of our yearning for a deeper connection with God. It is a spiritual odyssey where each step, each prayer, and each act of fasting carries the potential to transform not only the outer circumstances of our lives but also the inner landscape of our hearts.

> Taste and see that the Lord is good; blessed is the one who takes refuge in him.
>
> Psalm 34:8 (NIV)

As you embark on this journey, may you taste the goodness of the Lord in the moments of silence, in the pages of scripture, and in the surrender of fasting. May you find refuge in His presence, knowing that you are held in the arms of a loving and merciful God.

Throughout history, men and women of faith have discovered the power of fasting and prayer to break chains, heal wounds, and usher in seasons of divine favor. In their stories, we find echoes of our own spiritual yearnings and aspirations. Their testimonies become beacons, guiding us through the sometimes challenging terrain of our own spiritual pilgrimage.

Confidence in what we hope for and assurance about what we do not see.

Hebrews 11:1 (NIV)

Faith is As you journey through the pages of this book, may your faith be stirred, and may you walk with confidence in the unseen, trusting that your prayers are heard, and your fasting is seen by the One who sits enthroned above the heavens.

In the chapters ahead, we will explore the art of fasting, the beauty of prayer, and the synergy that occurs when these spiritual disciplines intertwine. Yet, beyond the practical guidance, may you encounter a deeper truth—that this journey is not about a set of rules or rituals but about a living relationship with the living God.

So, as we embark on this sacred expedition, let us do so with hearts open to the mystery, minds receptive to revelation, and spirits attuned to the gentle guidance of the Holy Spirit. May this book be a companion on your journey, a source of inspiration, and a catalyst for the transformative work that God desires to do in and through you.

May the grace of our Lord Jesus Christ, the love of God, and the communion of the Holy Spirit be with you now and throughout this sacred exploration. Amen.

Chapter 1

1.1. What Is Fasting

In the realm of spiritual disciplines, fasting stands as a timeless practice with roots embedded deep in the tapestry of human history. Across diverse cultures and religious traditions, fasting has been revered as a means of purification, self-discipline, and a pathway to heightened spiritual awareness. In this exploration, we delve into the multifaceted dimensions of fasting, understanding its essence, its historical significance, and its profound impact on the spiritual journey.

The Essence of Fasting

At its core, fasting is a deliberate act of abstaining from certain foods, drinks, or activities for a specified period. However, its significance extends far beyond the mere act of refraining from consumption. Fasting is a conscious choice to disconnect from the physical to engage with the spiritual, a symbolic gesture of surrender and reliance on a higher power.

1.   Fasting as a Spiritual Discipline

Fasting, in the context of spirituality, is a discipline that transcends the boundaries of religious affiliations. It is a universal language spoken by those seeking a deeper connection with the divine. Rooted in the belief that the physical act of refraining from sustenance opens channels for spiritual nourishment, fasting becomes a sacred pathway to encounter the transcendent.

2.   Surrender and Dependency:

Fasting underscores the principle of surrender, acknowledging our dependency on sustenance while deliberately choosing to prioritize spiritual nourishment. It is a tangible expression of the biblical truth found in Matthew 4:4:

> Man shall not live on bread alone, but on every word
> that comes from the mouth of God.
>
> Matthew 4:4 (NIV)

Through fasting, we embody this truth, recognizing that our existence is sustained not only by physical sustenance but by the spiritual sustenance derived from communion with God.

Types of Fasting

1.   Water Fasting:

Water fasting involves abstaining from all food and consuming only water for a specified period. It is often considered an intense form of fasting, and individuals undertaking water fasts typically prioritize rest and hydration.

2.   Partial Fasting:

Partial fasting involves restricting certain types of food or meals while maintaining a level of sustenance. This may include abstaining from specific food groups, such as meat, or adopting intermittent fasting patterns.

3.   Daniel Fast:

The Daniel Fast, inspired by the biblical account of Daniel's dietary choices (Daniel 1:8-14, NIV), involves consuming only fruits, vegetables, and water for a designated period. It is a spiritually focused fast emphasizing simplicity and reliance on plant-based foods.

The Spiritual Dynamics of Fasting

1.   Heightened Awareness:

Fasting acts as a catalyst for heightened spiritual awareness. When the distractions of daily sustenance are set aside, individuals often find their senses attuned to the whispers of the divine. The stillness cultivated through fasting creates a receptive space for spiritual insight and revelation.

2.   Discipline and Self-Control:

Fasting is a potent tool for cultivating discipline and self-control. The intentional act of denying the immediate gratification of physical desires fosters a robust inner discipline that extends beyond the fasting period. This aligns with the biblical exhortation in Galatians 5:22-23 (NIV) regarding the fruits of the Spirit, which include self-control.

3.   Humility and Dependence:

Fasting humbles the individual, acknowledging human frailty and dependence on God. The act of abstaining from sustenance is a tangible reminder that our strength comes not from self-sufficiency but from reliance on the Creator.

4.   Spiritual Warfare:

Fasting is recognized in many religious traditions as a form of spiritual warfare. It is a deliberate engagement in the battle between the flesh and the spirit, as articulated in Ephesians 6:12:

> For our struggle is not against flesh and blood, but against the rulers, against the authorities, against the powers of this dark world and against the spiritual forces of evil in the heavenly realms.
>
> Ephesians 6:12 (NIV)

Biblical Foundations of Fasting

1.   Jesus' Example:

The New Testament provides a profound example of fasting in the life of Jesus. In Matthew 4:1-2 (NIV), we read,

> Then Jesus was led by the Spirit into the wilderness to be tempted by the devil. After fasting forty days and forty nights, he was hungry.

Jesus' deliberate choice to fast for an extended period precedes a period of intense spiritual testing, demonstrating the spiritual fortitude that fasting can cultivate.

2.   Corporate Fasting:

Fasting is not only an individual practice but is also woven into the fabric of corporate worship and seeking God's guidance. In the book of Acts, we find instances of the early Christian community engaging in corporate fasting as they sought direction from the Holy Spirit (Acts 13:2-3, NIV).

3.   Spiritual Breakthrough:

Fasting is often associated with seeking spiritual breakthroughs. In situations of distress, uncertainty, or seeking divine intervention, individuals in the Bible turned to fasting as a means of earnestly seeking God's favor and guidance (Ezra 8:23, Joel 2:12, NIV).

Practical Considerations and Precautions

1.   Physical Health:

Before undertaking any form of fasting, individuals should consider their physical health. It is advisable to consult with healthcare professionals, especially for extended or rigorous fasts, to ensure that the body can safely endure the chosen fasting method.

2.   Gradual Transition:

For those new to fasting, a gradual transition is recommended.

i.   Begin with Shorter Fasts:

Starting with shorter fasts allows the body to adapt gradually. Consider beginning with intermittent fasting, where you abstain from food for a specific window of time, gradually extending the duration as your body adjusts.

ii.   Hydration:

Staying well-hydrated is paramount during fasting. Water is essential for bodily functions, and maintaining hydration helps mitigate potential side effects. As the Bible encourages:

> "The Lord will guide you always; he will satisfy your needs in a sun-scorched land and will strengthen your frame. You will be like a well-watered garden, like a spring whose waters never fail."
>
> Isaiah 58:11 (NIV)

iii.   Listen to Your Body:

Fasting is a personal journey, and it's crucial to listen to your body. If at any point you experience severe discomfort, dizziness, or other adverse effects, it's wise to break your fast and seek guidance from healthcare professionals.

iv.   Balanced Nutrition during Non-fasting Periods:

When not fasting, prioritize balanced nutrition to ensure the body receives essential nutrients. Consider incorporating a variety of fruits, vegetables, lean proteins, and whole grains into your meals.

Fasting and Prayer: A Symbiotic Relationship

1.   Deepening the Connection:

Fasting and prayer share a symbiotic relationship, each enhancing the efficacy of the other. As physical senses are subdued through fasting, the spiritual senses become heightened, facilitating a deeper connection with the divine.

2.   Seeking God's Guidance:

Throughout the Bible, fasting is intertwined with seeking God's guidance. In Acts 14:23, we read,

> Paul and Barnabas appointed elders for them in each
> church and, with prayer and fasting, committed them
> to the Lord, in whom they had put their trust.
>
> Acts 14:23 (NIV)

Fasting is a means of earnestly seeking divine direction and wisdom.

3.   Intimacy with God:

Fasting is a conduit for cultivating intimacy with God. In the stillness of fasting, individuals often find themselves drawn into a closer communion with the Creator. As Jesus declared

> But when you pray, go into your room, close the door and pray to your Father, who is unseen. Then your Father, who sees what is done in secret, will reward you.

> Matthew 6:6 (NIV)

4.   Intercessory Prayer:

Fasting is a powerful accompaniment to intercessory prayer. In times of collective need or when praying for others, fasting becomes a fervent expression of humility and dependency on God's intervention. The prophet Daniel, in chapter 9, engages in a period of fasting and prayer, seeking forgiveness and restoration for the people of Israel.

1.2.   When To Fast And Pray

Fasting and prayer are not isolated practices reserved for specific seasons; rather, they are dynamic spiritual disciplines that can be woven into the fabric of our lives. While there are traditional periods of fasting, such as Lent in Christianity or the month of Ramadan in Islam, the decision to fast and pray is deeply personal and can be prompted by a variety of circumstances. Let's explore when one might feel called to embark on this sacred journey.

- **Seeking Spiritual Guidance**

One of the most common reasons to fast and pray is when seeking spiritual guidance. In moments of indecision, confusion, or when facing significant life choices, individuals often turn to fasting as a means of seeking clarity from a higher source. As Proverbs 3:5-6 advises,

> Trust in the Lord with all your heart and lean not on your own understanding; in all your ways submit to him, and he will make your paths straight.
>
> Proverbs 3:5-6 (NIV)

- **During Times of Crisis**

In times of crisis, whether personal or collective, fasting and prayer can serve as a powerful response. It is a humble acknowledgment of our dependence on the divine in the face of challenges. Psalm 34:17-18 reassures,

> The righteous cry out, and the Lord hears them; he delivers them from all their troubles. The Lord is close to the brokenhearted and saves those who are crushed in spirit.
>
> Psalm 34:17-18 (NIV)

- **In Pursuit of Healing**

Fasting is often associated with physical and emotional healing. When grappling with illness, whether it be our own or that of a loved one, fasting becomes an act of surrender, seeking divine intervention for restoration and wholeness. James 5:14-15 encourages this practice:

> Is anyone among you sick? Let them call the elders of the church to pray over them and anoint them with oil in the name of the Lord. And the prayer offered in faith will make the sick person well.
>
> James 5:14-15 (NIV)

• Spiritual Breakthroughs

Individuals may feel led to fast and pray when pursuing spiritual breakthroughs. Whether overcoming persistent challenges, breaking free from spiritual strongholds, or seeking a deeper encounter with the Holy Spirit, fasting becomes a weapon in the spiritual arsenal. Ephesians 6:12 (NIV) acknowledges the spiritual battle:

> For our struggle is not against flesh and blood, but against the rulers, against the authorities, against the powers of this dark world and against the spiritual forces of evil in the heavenly realms.
>
> Ephesians 6:12 (NIV)

• In Times of Repentance

The act of fasting has deep roots in expressions of repentance. When individuals recognize the need for a turning point in their lives, a period of fasting and prayer can symbolize a sincere commitment to transformation. Joel 2:12 implores,

> "Even now," declares the Lord, 'return to me with all your heart, with fasting and weeping and mourning.
>
> Joel 2:12

- **During Discernment and Decision-Making**

When faced with major decisions, fasting becomes a way to surrender personal desires and seek alignment with God's will. By setting aside physical appetites, individuals create a space for discernment and divine guidance. Proverbs 16:9 reminds us,

> In their hearts humans plan their course, but the Lord establishes their steps.
>
> Proverbs 16:9 (NIV)

- **Communal Fasting**

Fasting is not solely an individual practice; it can also be a communal endeavor. When a community faces challenges, injustice, or collective repentance, communal fasting and prayer can unite hearts in seeking God's intervention. The book of Jonah portrays an entire city, Nineveh, fasting and turning to God in repentance.

- **Seasons of Gratitude**

Fasting need not always be associated with sorrow or need. Some individuals choose to fast as an expression of gratitude during seasons of abundance. It is a way to consecrate blessings and acknowledge the source of all good things. Fasting becomes an offering of thanks, recognizing that every good and perfect gift comes from above (James 1:17, NIV).

- **In Preparation for Spiritual Milestones**

Fasting is often observed as a preparation for significant spiritual milestones such as baptism, confirmation, or dedicating oneself to a specific ministry. It becomes a way of consecrating oneself before embarking on a new phase of the spiritual journey.

- **As a Regular Spiritual Discipline**

For some, fasting is incorporated into their regular spiritual disciplines. It becomes a rhythm of life—a conscious effort to cultivate self-discipline, maintain spiritual sensitivity, and foster an ongoing connection with the divine.

In essence, the decision to fast and pray is a deeply personal and spiritual one. It is guided by the inner prompting of the Holy Spirit, and the motivations may vary from seeking guidance to expressing gratitude. Ultimately, fasting is a response to the sacred moments and rhythms of life, an intentional pathway to draw near to the divine and align one's heart with the purposes of God. As Psalm 46:10 encourages,

Be still, and know that I am God.

Psalm 46:10 (NIV)

Fasting becomes a way to quiet the noise of the world and attune oneself to the presence of the Almighty.

1.3. Benefits Of Fasting And Prayers.

- **Spiritual Victory - Daniel's Fast:**

In the book of Daniel, we find a powerful example of fasting leading to spiritual victory. Daniel, along with his companions, undertook a fast, consuming only vegetables and water. As a result, they experienced not only physical well-being but also spiritual favor, wisdom, and understanding (Daniel 1:8-17, NIV).

- **Guidance and Deliverance - Esther's Fast:**

Queen Esther, facing a grave threat to her people, declared a fast among the Jews in Susa before approaching King Xerxes. This collective fast sought divine guidance and deliverance, leading to a turn of events that preserved the Jewish people from destruction (Esther 4:15-17, NIV).

- **Repentance and Mercy - Nineveh's Fast:**

The city of Nineveh, in response to the prophetic message of Jonah, proclaimed a fast and turned to God in repentance. Their collective fasting and prayers led to God's mercy, and the city was spared from the impending judgment (Jonah 3:5-10, NIV).

- **Spiritual Insight - Jesus' 40-Day Fast:**

Before commencing His public ministry, Jesus fasted for 40 days and nights in the wilderness. This period of intense fasting and prayer resulted in spiritual insight, resilience against temptation, and preparation for the ministry ahead (Matthew 4:1-11, NIV).

- **Healing and Restoration - King David's Fast:**

In times of personal distress, King David engaged in fasting and prayers for the healing and restoration of his sick child. Despite the child's eventual passing, David's fasting reflected a deep dependence on God's mercy and grace (2 Samuel 12:15-23, NIV).

- **Spiritual Breakthrough - Apostle Paul's Fast:**

The Apostle Paul, during his missionary journeys, often engaged in fasting and prayers. In Acts 13, while the church in Antioch was fasting, the Holy Spirit spoke, commissioning Paul and Barnabas for the work of spreading the Gospel (Acts 13:2-3, NIV).

- **Seeking God's Will - Cornelius' Fast:**

Cornelius, a devout Gentile, fasted and prayed, seeking God's will and righteousness. His sincere seeking caught God's attention, leading to a divine encounter with the Apostle Peter and the subsequent inclusion of the Gentiles in the early Christian community (Acts 10:30-33, NIV).

- **Overcoming Spiritual Opposition - Ezra's Fast:**

In the book of Ezra, we find a communal fast undertaken in response to the spiritual challenges faced by the returning exiles. The fasting and prayers resulted in divine protection and guidance, overcoming opposition and ensuring the success of their mission (Ezra 8:21-23, NIV).

- **Spiritual Unity - Pentecost's Fast:**

Before the Day of Pentecost, the disciples were in unity, devoting themselves to prayer and fasting. This spiritual preparation set the stage for the outpouring of the Holy Spirit and the birth of the early Christian Church (Acts 1:14, NIV).

- **Renewal and Repentance - Nehemiah's Fast:**

Nehemiah, upon hearing about the state of Jerusalem, fasted, mourned, and prayed for renewal and restoration. His fasting and prayers played a crucial role in the rebuilding of Jerusalem's walls and the spiritual revival of the people (Nehemiah 1:4-11, NIV).

Chapter 2

Understanding The word Decree

A decree is a resolute and unshakable proclamation, an exercise of power through authoritative words and commands, bearing a near certainty of fulfillment. It can also manifest as an order equivalent in force to law. Additionally, a decree can be a religious ordinance established by a council or a particular authority, serving as a means through which predetermined intentions are set. Comparable to a judgment pronounced in a probate court affirming a judicial order, decrees vary, encompassing both positive and negative declarations.

God, the ultimate initiator of decrees, imparts the power of decree to those who believe in Him. The creation of all entities—be it the heavens, angels, sun, moon, stars, or light—is a result of God's decree.

> Praise ye him, all his angels: praise ye him, all his hosts. Praise ye him, sun and moon: praise him, all ye stars of light. Praise him, you highest heavens and you waters above the skies. Let them praise the name of the Lord, for at his command they were created, He hath also stablished them for ever and ever: he hath made a decree which shall not pass.

> Psalm 148:2-6

Notably, both God and believers possess the authority to issue decrees. As God's creation, believers are bestowed with the right to command elements and elemental powers, expecting obedience from the moon, sun, and stars. However, adversaries exploit this power for malevolent

34

purposes, using decrees against God's people. Believers are encouraged to make decrees in alignment with God's principles, standing firm against opposition.

> By me kings reign, and princes decree justice. When he gave to the sea his decree, that the waters should not pass his commandment: when he appointed the foundations of the earth.

Proverbs 8:15, 29

God's decrees are enduring, and believers are encouraged to exhibit a similar unwavering stance. Despite initial challenges or opposing circumstances, a believer's decree, rooted in faith, is expected to stand firm. Jeremiah 5:22 illustrates this steadfastness:

> Fear ye not me? saith the Lord: will ye not tremble at my presence, which have placed the sand for the bound of the sea by a perpetual decree, that it cannot pass it: and though the waves thereof toss themselves, yet can they not prevail; though they roar, yet can they not pass over it?

Jeremiah 5:22

The efficacy of decrees is attested by biblical figures such as Daniel, Esther, and Cornelius, who experienced divine intervention through their faithful proclamations. Believers are urged to emulate their faith, understanding that when God is involved in a decree, adversaries must yield. Job 22:28 emphasizes the believer's power to decree:

Thou shalt also decree a thing, and it shall be established unto thee: and the light shall shine upon thy ways.

Job 22:28

This power is emphasized further, asserting that when a believer revokes an evil decree through prayer or fasting, light will illuminate their path, dispelling darkness.

Faith, integral to the process of decreeing, has been demonstrated throughout biblical history. Hebrews 11:2-3 highlights the role of faith in obtaining favorable outcomes. The persistence of Moses' prayers, answered centuries later, underscores the enduring nature of decrees made in faith.

Believers are encouraged not to relent in decreeing positive outcomes in their lives. The spoken words of a true believer carry the potency of decrees, capable of shaping destinies and overcoming challenges. Whether in times of trouble or seasons of prosperity, believers are reminded of their authority to speak into existence the will of God for their lives.

Chapter 3

Preparation Section for Fasting and Prayer

21 Prayers for Strength During Fasting

Fasting is a spiritual discipline that involves abstaining from food or certain activities for a specific period, often undertaken for deeper communion with God, seeking spiritual strength, and discerning His guidance. This topic focuses on 21 heartfelt prayers aimed at seeking strength, resilience, and divine support during the period of fasting. These prayers cover various aspects of the fasting journey, including physical strength, spiritual insight, perseverance, and an unwavering connection with God.

"But those who hope in the Lord will renew their strength. They will soar on wings like eagles; they will run and not grow weary, they will walk and not be faint." This verse highlights the promise of renewed strength for those who place their trust in the Lord during challenging times.

Isaiah 40:31 (NIV)

"I can do all this through him who gives me strength." Paul's affirmation in this verse underscores the believer's capacity to endure and persevere through the strength derived from Christ.

Philippians 4:13 (NIV)

Prayer Points

1. Heavenly Father, grant me physical strength to endure the rigors of fasting; let weakness be replaced by Your divine vitality, in Jesus' name.

2. Lord, as I fast, infuse me with spiritual discernment to hear Your voice clearly and receive guidance for the journey ahead, in Jesus' name.

3. I pray for resilience in the face of challenges during this fast; let every obstacle become an opportunity for spiritual growth, in Jesus' name.

4. Father, empower me to resist the distractions that may divert my focus from seeking You wholeheartedly during this fasting period, in Jesus' name.

5. I decree supernatural endurance to press on when the journey feels tough; let Your grace sustain me, in Jesus' name.

6. Lord, fortify my mind against doubts and negative thoughts; let Your peace guard my heart and mind, in Jesus' name.

7. I pray for a deep hunger and thirst for Your Word and presence; let my soul be satisfied in You alone, in Jesus' name.

8. Heavenly Father, let this fasting period be a time of spiritual purification and sanctification; cleanse me from within, in Jesus' name.

9. I rebuke every spirit of weariness and fatigue; I receive divine energy and vitality, in Jesus' name.

10. Lord, grant me wisdom to prioritize prayer and communion with You over worldly distractions, in Jesus' name.

11. I break the chains of unhealthy habits and cravings; let this fasting period bring about lasting transformation, in Jesus' name.

12. Father, align my desires with Yours during this fast; let Your will be my priority, in Jesus' name.

13. I pray for emotional strength to navigate the ups and downs of this fasting journey; let Your joy be my strength, in Jesus' name.

14. Lord, surround me with a community of believers for mutual encouragement and support during this fast, in Jesus' name.

15. I declare victory over every spiritual opposition that may attempt to hinder my fasting experience; I am more than a conqueror, in Jesus' name.

16. Heavenly Father, deepen my intimacy with You during this time of fasting; let my relationship with You flourish, in Jesus' name.

17. I release forgiveness and let go of any bitterness or resentment; cleanse my heart as I seek Your forgiveness, in Jesus' name.

18. I pray for a spirit of gratitude and thanksgiving to prevail in my heart throughout this fasting period, in Jesus' name.

19. Lord, reveal Your purpose and direction for my life as I seek Your face in fasting and prayer, in Jesus' name.

20. Father, let the fruits of the Spirit—love, joy, peace—abound in me during this fast, in Jesus' name.

21. I declare that as I seek You with sincerity during this fasting period, I will emerge stronger, transformed, and closer to Your heart, in Jesus' name.

Affirmation Prayers

I affirm that during this season of fasting, I am strengthened by the power of God. My spirit, soul, and body align with the divine purpose of this fast, and I walk in the assurance that God's grace sustains me. Every prayer uttered with sincerity is heard, and I emerge from this period with increased spiritual resilience, clarity, and a deeper connection with my Heavenly Father. In Jesus' name, I receive the strength needed for this journey of fasting and emerge victorious on the other side. Amen.

Prayers
Section

Chapter 4

Prayer for Divine Protection and Security

In the ebb and flow of life's unpredictable currents, our hearts often yearn for a sanctuary, a shield that transcends the material realm—a divine refuge where safety and security intertwine with the rhythm of our existence. This prayer for divine protection and security is an emotional plea, a heartfelt cry to the Almighty, recognizing that within the vast tapestry of our vulnerabilities, God stands as an unwavering fortress.

> "Whoever dwells in the shelter of the Most High will rest in the shadow of the Almighty. I will say of the Lord, 'He is my refuge and my fortress, my God, in whom I trust."
>
> Psalm 91:1-2 (NIV)

In the hallowed words of Psalm 91, we find solace—a poetic embrace that cradles us in the assurance of God's shelter. As we lift our voices in prayer, we echo the sentiment that dwelling in the Most High is not just a physical proximity but a spiritual cocoon where fears dissipate in the radiance of divine love.

This prayer becomes an emotional odyssey—a plea for protection against the storms that assail us, whether they be the tempests of the tangible world or the subtle whispers of spiritual warfare. The language we use is not just a string of words but an outpouring of our deepest fears and our most fervent desires for safety.

> "The Lord will keep you from all harm—he will watch over your life; the Lord will watch over your coming and going both now and forevermore."

Here, the emotional tenor deepens as we contemplate the profound promise that the Lord keeps vigilant watch over every facet of our existence. The prayer unfolds as a plea not just for temporal security but for an enduring embrace that transcends the boundaries of time.

Our emotional entreaty rises as we acknowledge the fragility of our mortal journey. We beseech divine protection not only in the grand moments of life but in the minutiae of our daily comings and goings. This prayer resonates with the raw emotion of a soul seeking a haven, a sanctuary where vulnerability meets omnipotence.

As we utter each word, it's not merely a recitation but a soul-stirring communion—an emotional dialogue with the Creator, trusting that our vulnerability is met with a divine security that surpasses understanding. In the midst of life's uncertainties, this prayer becomes a testament to our unwavering belief that God's protection is not just a request but a divine assurance, wrapping us in an emotional embrace that whispers, "You are safe, my child."

4.1. Prayer to Return to Divine Protection

1. Heavenly Father, in Your warmth, I find solace. Guide me through life's complexities, enveloping me in Your protective love and grace, in Jesus' name.

2. Lord, forgive my moments of straying. Lead me back to the shelter of Your wings, where fear gives way to faith, in Jesus' name.

3. Father, I surrender my vulnerabilities. Weave a divine shield, guarding me from doubts and insecurity, in Jesus' name.

4. In my weaknesses, I cry for Your strength. Lift me from uncertainty, restoring my soul to Your care, in Jesus' name.

5. Lord, amidst life's noise, tune my heart to Your protection. Let harmony replace discord, and peace reign, in Jesus' name.

6. Be my shield in life's storms. Lead me to trust, where fear flees before Your divine protection, in Jesus' name.

7. Forgive my self-reliance. I seek refuge in Your wings, where weaknesses find strength and insecurities drown in Your love, in Jesus' name.

8. In brokenness, I need Your covering. Bind me to Your promises, where fractures mend, and wounds heal, in Jesus' name.

9. Sovereign God, redirect my focus to Your lighthouse. Still life's turbulent waves, illuminating the path with Your guidance, in Jesus' name.

10. Tune my heart to Your presence amidst distractions. Let Your protection orchestrate my steps, harmonizing my journey with Your love, in Jesus' name.

11. Lord, precede and follow me with Your protection. Be my strength where I'm weak, my guide where I falter, leading me back to Your sanctuary, in Jesus' name.

12. In this prayer, I plead for a return to Your protection. May Your arms enfold me, and Your grace accompany every step, in Jesus' name.

4.2. Prayer for Divine Guidance

1. Heavenly Father, in life's maze, I feel uncertainty. Guide me back to Your divine guidance. Let Your light pierce shadows, leading me with clarity, in Jesus' name.

2. Lord, as I reflect on faltering steps, I need Your unfailing guidance. Steer me from indecision into Your purpose, in Jesus' name.

3. Father, align the compass of my heart with Your will. Lead me back to Your divine guidance, where confusion transforms into certainty, in Jesus' name.

4. In doubts, I cry out for Your wisdom. Let Your guidance be a beacon, illuminating the way to Your perfect will, in Jesus' name.

5. Lord, I long for Your voice. Amidst competing voices, attune my ears to Your guidance, where assurance replaces anxiety, in Jesus' name.

6. As I stand at crossroads, be my guiding star. Lead me back to Your purpose, where every step is marked by Your divine guidance, in Jesus' name.

7. Forgive my self-reliance. I seek Your guidance, where self-doubt is replaced by confidence in following Your lead, in Jesus' name.

8. In my plans, I surrender to Your hands. Piece together a roadmap of divine guidance, ordered by Your sovereign will, in Jesus' name.

9. Sovereign God, redirect my steps to Your guidance. Let clarity reign at the intersection of Your divine guidance, in Jesus' name.

10. Amidst life's demands, tune my heart to Your guidance. Let Your wisdom orchestrate my decisions, harmonizing with Your love, in Jesus' name.

11. Lord, as I navigate uncharted waters, be my compass. Let Your guidance be the north star orienting my journey, in Jesus' name.

12. In this prayer, I anchor my plea for a return to Your divine guidance. May Your voice be the compass that directs me, in Jesus' name.

4.3. Prayer for Divine Security

1. Heavenly Father, enfold me in the haven of Your divine security, where my fears are hushed by the whispers of Your steadfast love, in Jesus' name.

2. Lord, carve out a sanctuary within Your embrace, shielding me from the tempests of life with the fortress of Your divine security, in Jesus' name.

3. In the trembling moments of my heart, I cry out for Your unwavering protection. May Your divine security be a radiant shield against the shadows that seek to engulf me, in Jesus' name.

4. Sovereign God, let Your love be the anchor that secures me in the storm. Wrap me in the cocoon of Your divine security, where anxiety surrenders to the tranquility of Your presence, in Jesus' name.

5. Amidst the echoes of uncertainty, I seek refuge in Your unwavering arms. Be my fortress, O Lord, and let Your divine security stand as an impenetrable barrier against the uncertainties that assail me, in Jesus' name.

6. Father, in the turbulence of life, be my anchor. May Your divine security hold me steadfast, preventing the currents of doubt from sweeping me away, in Jesus' name.

7. As I face the unknown, I plead for Your protective wings to overshadow me. Let Your divine security be my refuge, shielding me from the arrows of despair, in Jesus' name.

8. Lord, in the fragility of my humanity, I surrender to Your divine security. May Your love be the unyielding fortress that guards me from the vulnerabilities of life, in Jesus' name.

9. In the whispers of the night, I call upon Your name for security. Let Your divine presence stand as a guardian, dispelling the shadows of fear with the radiant light of Your assurance, in Jesus' name.

10. Heavenly Father, carve out a safe haven within Your heart for my weary soul. Let Your divine security be a beacon that guides me through the darkness, in Jesus' name.

11. As I navigate the uncertainties, I implore You to be my anchor and shield. May Your divine security be a fortress of strength, where weakness is replaced by the resilience of Your enduring love, in Jesus' name.

12. Lord, engrave Your promises on the tablet of my heart. Let Your divine security be an unshakeable foundation, a refuge where my trust finds its home, in Jesus' name.

Chapter 5

Prayer for The Next Level

Do not be anxious about anything, but in every situation, by prayer and petition, with thanksgiving, present your requests to God. And the peace of God, which transcends all understanding, will guard your hearts and your minds in Christ Jesus.

Philippians 4:6-7 (NIV)

5.1. Prayer to Break Free from Evil Patterns

1. Heavenly Father, liberate me from chains of evil patterns. Break every hindrance to spiritual growth, guiding me into Your light, in Jesus' name.

2. Lord, break shackles binding me to repeated mistakes. Guide me onto the path of righteousness and freedom, in Jesus' name.

3. In silence, I seek Your intervention. Break generational curses perpetuating evil patterns. Let Your mercy pave the way to transformation, in Jesus' name.

4. Father, break me free from cycles of sin and darkness. Shatter the stronghold of evil patterns, bringing me into the liberty of Your love, in Jesus' name.

5. Sovereign Lord, grant strength to break cycles of temptation. Surge Your power through me, shattering bonds of these evil patterns, in Jesus' name.

6. In emotional depth, I confess my need for deliverance. Break invisible chains binding me to destructive habits, freeing me to abundant life, in Jesus' name.

7. Lord, break the yoke of recurring patterns. Replace it with Your gentle guidance, leading me from darkness into the light of Your love, in Jesus' name.

8. In the battlefield of my mind, break the cycle of negative thoughts and behaviors. Let Your truth demolish every stronghold of evil patterns, in Jesus' name.

9. Heavenly Father, break the cycle of self-condemnation. Replace it with assurance of Your forgiveness and grace. Let Your love restore my soul, in Jesus' name.

10. As I confront threatening patterns, I plead for Your intervention. Break the cycle of stagnation, propelling me forward into a deeper relationship with You, in Jesus' name.

11. Lord, break the cycle of fear and anxiety. Fill the void with peace that surpasses understanding. Let Your love be the antidote to every toxic pattern, in Jesus' name.

12. In fervency, I declare dependence on Your transformative power. Break chains of addiction, bondage, and sinful cycles, ushering me into the freedom of Your redeeming love, in Jesus' name.

5.2. Prayer to Resist Reverting to Square One

1. Heavenly Father, strengthen my spirit to resist the allure of familiar but destructive paths. Grant courage to break free from regression, in Jesus' name.

2. Lord, guard my heart against the temptation to return to square one. May Your grace shield me from old habits, in Jesus' name.

3. In the emotional battleground, break the cycle of self-doubt. Grant resilience to move forward, resisting the pull of the past, in Jesus' name.

4. Sovereign God, lift me above the shadows of my past. I resist reverting to square one, clinging to the promise of Your redemption, in Jesus' name.

5. Father, strengthen my resolve to resist the pull of old patterns. Let Your love anchor me in the journey of growth, in Jesus' name.

6. In this prayer, lead me away from stagnation. Propel me towards the fullness of Your purpose. I resist regression and embrace progress, in Jesus' name.

7. Lord, piece my past mistakes into a mosaic of grace. May Your mercy propel me forward, resisting the allure of what's left behind, in Jesus' name.

8. In emotional surrender, break the chains binding me to the past. Grant strength to resist reverting to square one, trusting in Your transformation, in Jesus' name.

9. Heavenly Father, be my compass. Guard me against detours leading back to square one. I resist regression and choose the journey of faith, in Jesus' name.

10. Lord, break cycles of complacency and fear. Grant tenacity to resist any pull back to square one, in Jesus' name.

11. Father, guide me away from pitfalls of the past. I resist the gravitational force of regression, embracing the upward call, in Jesus' name.

12. In this sanctuary, declare victory over fear. Let Your love propel me forward. I resist reverting to square one, choosing renewal and transformation, in Jesus' name.

5.3. Prayer to Move from Poverty to Prosperity

1. Heavenly Father, lift my eyes from need to abundance. Break poverty's chains, ushering me into prosperity, a divine shift in Jesus' name.

2. Lord, at the threshold of lack, surrendering financial struggles. Let rivers of prosperity flow, turning poverty into abundance, in Jesus' name.

3. In emotional depth, confess longing for financial brightness. Break scarcity's cycles, opening floodgates of prosperity. Trust in Your provision, in Jesus' name.

4. Sovereign God, like a seed in barren soil, entrust financial situation. Break through lack, nurturing prosperity's seeds. End poverty, begin abundance, in Jesus' name.

5. Father, navigating financial strain, seek Your intervention. Break barriers to poverty, release blessings of prosperity. Receive abundance with gratitude, in Jesus' name.

6. In emotional sanctuary, declare faith in Your prosperity promise. Break financial hardship's grip, lead into abundance's spacious land. Resist poverty, embrace ordained prosperity, in Jesus' name.

7. Lord, offer financial struggles. Break chains of lack, release Your provision's wealth. May the journey testify to Your faithfulness, from poverty to prosperity, in Jesus' name.

8. Heavenly Father, surrender financial concerns. Break scarcity's cycles, pour out Your prosperity. Receive blessings with an open heart, in Jesus' name.

9. Standing on the precipice of financial breakthrough, plead for Your favor. Break walls confining to poverty, open doors of prosperity. Trust in divine reversal, in Jesus' name.

10. Lord, in emotional vulnerability, cast financial anxieties. Break poverty's spirit, let prosperity's dawn illuminate. Declare a shift from lack to abundance, in Jesus' name.

11. Father, weary traveler in financial desert, seeking an oasis. Break drought of poverty, let streams of prosperity flow. Receive bountiful provision with gratitude, in Jesus' name.

12. In sanctuary, declare trust in Your transformation. Break cycles of poverty, lead into unprecedented prosperity. Receive divine shift with faith, in Jesus' name.

Chapter 6

Prayer Against Sickness, Death, And Infirmities

But I will restore you to health and heal your wounds, declares the Lord because you are called an outcast, Zion for whom no one cares.

Jeremiah 30:17 (NIV)

6.1. Prayer to Eliminate Infirmities

1. Heavenly Father, in my pain, I plead for Your healing touch. Break the chains of infirmity binding my body; I declare freedom, in Jesus' name.

2. Lord, in my weakness, I surrender my health to Your care. Break the cycle of infirmity; I receive Your restoring touch, in Jesus' name.

3. In quiet moments, I confess dependence on Your mercy. Break the grip of infirmities, replacing it with Your healing grace, in Jesus' name.

4. Sovereign God, like a vessel needing repair, I submit to Your hands. Break patterns of sickness; fill me with completeness, in Jesus' name.

5. Father, in physical challenges, implore Your intervention. Break chains of infirmity; let Your miraculous healing flow, in Jesus' name.

6. In this sanctuary of faith, I resist every ailment. Break bonds of infirmities; envelop me in Your warmth, in Jesus' name.

7. Lord, I offer my weaknesses; break chains hindering me. Release strength from Your divine touch; I receive Your healing, in Jesus' name.

8. Heavenly Father, in pain, I surrender health concerns. Break cycles of infirmity; let Your healing light shine, in Jesus' name.

9. On the brink of healing, I plead for favor. Break strongholds; grant a divine turnaround, in Jesus' name.

10. Lord, in vulnerability, I cast health anxieties at Your feet. Break the spirit of infirmity; I declare freedom, in Jesus' name.

11. Father, offering my body, I pray for Your cleansing touch. Break chains of infirmity; I resist every ailment, in Jesus' name.

12. In my need, I declare victory over infirmities. Break every stronghold; fill me with vitality, in Jesus' name.

6.2. Prayer Against Recurrent Afflictions

1. Heavenly Father, amidst relentless trials, I seek Your refuge. Break the chains of recurrent afflictions threatening to overwhelm me. I declare freedom, in Jesus' name.

2. Lord, facing persistent challenges, I surrender battles to Your victorious hand. Break the cycle of afflictions; let Your healing power reign in my life, in Jesus' name.

3. In quiet moments, I lay weariness before You. Break the grip of recurring trials, replacing it with strength from Your divine intervention. I resist afflictions, in Jesus' name.

4. Sovereign God, like a weary traveler, I turn to Your refuge. Break patterns of recurrent afflictions; let Your peace soothe my soul. I declare victory over these cycles, in Jesus' name.

5. Father, navigating the storm of challenges, I implore Your intervention. Break chains of recurrent afflictions; release miraculous healing. I trust in Your power to end these cycles, in Jesus' name.

6. In the emotional sanctuary of this prayer, I declare unwavering faith in Your promise of deliverance. Break bondages of afflictions; let streams of restoration flow. I resist every persistent trial, in Jesus' name.

7. Lord, I offer weariness to Your authority. Break chains of recurrent afflictions; release strength from Your divine touch. I receive deliverance with open arms, in Jesus' name.

8. Heavenly Father, in the quietude of struggles, I surrender recurrent challenges to Your care. Break cycles of afflictions; let Your deliverance shine. I receive freedom, in Jesus' name.

9. As I stand on the brink of breakthrough, I plead for Your favor. Break strongholds of afflictions; grant a divine turnaround. I trust in Your miraculous intervention, in Jesus' name.

10. Lord, in emotional vulnerability, I cast burdens at Your feet. Break the spirit of afflictions lingering, and let the dawn of complete deliverance illuminate my path. I declare victory, in Jesus' name.

11. Father, offering struggles, I pray for Your cleansing touch. Break chains of afflictions; let Your deliverance power surge through me. I resist every persistent trial and claim victory, in Jesus' name.

12. In the depths of need, I declare triumph over afflictions. Break strongholds; fill me with peace and deliverance from Your divine touch. I receive freedom, in Jesus' name.

6.3. Prayer to Halt Borrowing and Death

1. Heavenly Father, in my financial struggles, break the cycle of borrowing weighing on me. I declare an end to financial bondage, in Jesus' name.

2. Lord, facing debts, I surrender my financial burdens. Break the chains of borrowing that suffocate me. I declare financial freedom, in Jesus' name.

3. In quiet moments, I confess financial dependence on Your mercy. Break the grip of borrowing; release divine provision. I resist the cycle of debt, in Jesus' name.

4. Sovereign God, like a weary traveler, I turn to Your guidance. Break patterns of financial struggle and borrowing, replacing them with Your abundance. I declare an end to financial despair, in Jesus' name.

5. Father, navigating financial challenges, I implore Your intervention. Break chains of borrowing; release miraculous provision. I trust in Your power to lift me from financial despair, in Jesus' name.

6. In this emotional sanctuary, I declare unwavering faith in Your promise of financial deliverance. Break bondages of borrowing; let Your abundance flow. I resist the grip of financial lack, in Jesus' name.

7. Lord, I offer financial struggles to Your authority. Break chains of borrowing; release financial stability. I receive Your provision with open arms, in Jesus' name.

8. Heavenly Father, in my financial challenges, I surrender to Your loving care. Break cycles of borrowing; let Your provision shine. I receive financial breakthrough, in Jesus' name.

9. Standing on the brink of financial relief, I plead for Your favor. Break strongholds of borrowing; grant a divine turnaround. I trust in Your miraculous provision, in Jesus' name.

10. Lord, in emotional vulnerability, I cast financial anxieties at Your feet. Break the spirit of borrowing; let the dawn of complete financial deliverance illuminate my path. I declare victory over financial struggles, in Jesus' name.

11. Father, offering financial concerns, I pray for Your prosperous touch. Break chains of borrowing; let Your provision power surge through every aspect of my financial life. I resist every cycle of financial lack, in Jesus' name.

12. In the depths of financial need, I declare triumph over borrowing. Break every stronghold of financial struggles; fill me with the abundance from Your divine touch. I receive financial breakthrough, in Jesus' name.

6.4. Prayer to Remove Death Traps

1. Heavenly Father, in life's shadows, break snares set for harm or death. I declare divine protection, in Jesus' name.

2. Lord, facing unseen perils, surrender safety. Break enemy plans for deadly traps. I declare Your deliverance, in Jesus' name.

3. In quiet moments, confess dependence on Your mercy. Break darkness' strategies to set death traps. Resist hidden danger, in Jesus' name.

4. Sovereign God, navigating uncertainties, implore Your intervention. Break hidden snares set by the adversary. Declare freedom from deadly plots, in Jesus' name.

5. Father, in emotional sanctuary, declare unwavering faith. Break every death trap. Resist every form of harm, in Jesus' name.

6. Lord, offer safety to Your sovereign authority. Break enemy plans for death traps. Receive Your shield of protection, in Jesus' name.

7. Heavenly Father, in life's quietude, surrender well-being. Break hidden traps; let Your protection shine. Receive divine safety, in Jesus' name.

8. Standing on brink of danger, plead for favor. Break every death trap; grant divine turnaround in safety. Trust in miraculous intervention, in Jesus' name.

9. Lord, in emotional vulnerability, cast safety concerns. Break every trap; let complete protection illuminate. Declare victory over hidden danger, in Jesus' name.

10. Father, offering safety, pray for watchful eye. Break every snare and trap. Resist every form of harm, in Jesus' name.

11. In need of protection, declare triumph over death traps. Break every danger; fill with assurance of divine safety. Receive Your shield, in Jesus' name.

12. Heavenly Father, amidst dangers, break harm and death cycles. Declare divine safety, in Jesus' name.

13. Lord, facing unforeseen dangers, break chains of harm and death. Declare Your deliverance, in Jesus' name.

14. In quiet moments, confess dependence on Your mercy. Break darkness' strategies to set death traps. Resist hidden danger, in Jesus' name.

15. Sovereign God, navigating uncertainties, break hidden snares. Declare freedom from every deadly plot, in Jesus' name.

6.5.   Prayer for Victory Over Sin, Sickness, and Diseases

1. Heavenly Father, in the battle against sin, sickness, and diseases, I lift my heart to You. Break every chain; grant victory over strongholds. I declare triumph, in Jesus' name.

2. Lord, facing shadows of infirmity, I surrender my health to Your healing touch. Break sickness and disease; let Your restoration power flow. I declare victory, in Jesus' name.

3. In quiet moments, I confess dependence on Your mercy. Break sin's strongholds; grant victory over every temptation. I resist bondage, in Jesus' name.

4. Sovereign God, navigating life's challenges, implore Your intervention. Break sickness and diseases' chains; release miraculous healing. I declare victory, in Jesus' name.

5. Father, in emotional sanctuary, declare unwavering faith in Your promise of deliverance. Break hindering sin; let Your grace abound. I resist illness, in Jesus' name.

6. Lord, offer struggles to Your sovereign authority. Break sin, sickness, and disease chains hindering well-being. I receive Your victory, in Jesus' name.

7. Heavenly Father, in life's quietude, surrender battles to Your loving care. Break cycles of sin, sickness, and diseases; let Your victory reign. I declare freedom, in Jesus' name.

8. Standing on brink of potential defeat, plead for favor. Break every stronghold; grant a divine turnaround. Trust in miraculous intervention, in Jesus' name.

9. Lord, in emotional vulnerability, cast burdens at Your feet. Break sin and sickness spirit; let complete deliverance illuminate. I declare victory, in Jesus' name.

10. Father, offering battles, pray for Your cleansing touch. Break sin, sickness, and diseases chains; let Your victory power surge. I resist bondage, in Jesus' name.

11. In the depths of need for deliverance, declare triumph. Break every sin and sickness stronghold; fill with victorious divine touch. I receive freedom, in Jesus' name.

12. Heavenly Father, amidst the battle, break defeat cycles. Declare Your victory over every area of my life, in Jesus' name.

13. Lord, facing shadows of infirmity, break health-binding chains. Declare Your healing victory, in Jesus' name.

14. In quiet moments, confess dependence on Your mercy. Break sin strongholds; grant victory over every temptation. I resist bondage, in Jesus' name.

15. Sovereign God, navigating life's challenges, break sickness and diseases chains. Declare victorious healing, in Jesus' name.

6.6. Prayer for Victory Over Death

1. Heavenly Father, facing life's end, I turn to Your mercy. Break fear of death; grant victory over its sting. I declare triumph, in Jesus' name.

2. Lord, facing mortality's shadows, I surrender my soul. Break death's hold; let Your promise of life prevail. I declare victory, in Jesus' name.

3. In quiet moments, confess dependence on Your mercy. Break fear of death; grant assurance of eternal life. I resist despair, in Jesus' name.

4. Sovereign God, navigating mortality, implore Your intervention. Break fear and uncertainty of death; release hope of eternal glory. I declare victory, in Jesus' name.

5. Father, in emotional sanctuary, declare unwavering faith in Your promise. Break every fear; let assurance of eternal life reign. I resist doubt, in Jesus' name.

6. Lord, offer my soul to Your authority. Break death's grip; let the promise of resurrection bring peace. I receive Your victory, in Jesus' name.

7. Heavenly Father, in quietude, surrender eternity to Your care. Break fear of death's separation; let joy of eternal reunion prevail. I declare freedom, in Jesus' name.

8. Standing on brink of mortality, plead for favor. Break anxiety; grant divine assurance of victory over death. I trust in miraculous intervention, in Jesus' name.

9. Lord, in emotional vulnerability, cast fears at Your feet. Break spirit of despair; let dawn of complete victory illuminate. I declare triumph, in Jesus' name.

10. Father, offering my soul, pray for Your comforting touch. Break fear's chains; let victory of eternal life resonate. I resist uncertainty, in Jesus' name.

11. In depths of need for assurance, declare triumph over fear of death. Break every stronghold; fill with victory from Your promise. I receive freedom, in Jesus' name.

12. Heavenly Father, amidst contemplation of life's end, break cycle of fear and uncertainty. Declare Your victory over fear of death, in Jesus' name.

13. Lord, facing shadows of mortality, break chains binding my soul. Declare promise of eternal life, in Jesus' name.

14. In quiet moments, confess dependence on Your mercy. Break fear of death's unknown; grant assurance of eternal life. I resist despair, in Jesus' name.

15. Sovereign God, navigating reality of mortality, break fear and uncertainty of death. Declare victorious promise of eternal life, in Jesus' name.

Chapter 7

Prayer Against Bondages

It is for freedom that Christ has set us free. Stand firm, then, and do not let yourselves be burdened again by a yoke of slavery.

Galatians 5:1 (NIV)

He brought them out of darkness, the utter darkness, and broke away their chains.

Psalm 107:14 (NIV)

7.1. Anointing for Breaking Sexual Bondage

1. Lord, break chains of sexual bondage in my life. Anoint me for purity and freedom, in Jesus' name.

2. Heavenly Father, release me from the grip of sexual bondage. Anoint me for holiness, in Jesus' name.

3. Break every stronghold of sexual bondage. Anoint me with purity, in Jesus' name.

4. Father, set me free from the shackles of sexual bondage. Anoint me with Your cleansing power, in Jesus' name.

5. Lord, break the ties of sexual bondage. Anoint me for victorious purity, in Jesus' name.

6. Heavenly Father, dismantle every chain of sexual bondage. Anoint me with Your liberating grace, in Jesus' name.

7. Break the yoke of sexual bondage in my life. Anoint me for purity, in Jesus' name.

8. Father, release me from the bondage of impurity. Anoint me with Your sanctifying power, in Jesus' name.

9. Lord, break the grip of sexual sin. Anoint me for victorious purity, in Jesus' name.

10. Heavenly Father, dismantle every chain of sexual bondage. Anoint me for freedom, in Jesus' name.

11. Break the strongholds of sexual bondage. Anoint me with Your cleansing power, in Jesus' name.

12. Father, set me free from the chains of sexual bondage. Anoint me with Your liberating grace, in Jesus' name.

13. Lord, break the power of sexual sin. Anoint me with Your sanctifying power, in Jesus' name.

14. Heavenly Father, release me from the grip of sexual bondage. Anoint me for purity, in Jesus' name.

15. Break every stronghold of sexual bondage. Anoint me with victorious purity, in Jesus' name.

7.2. Prayer to Break Free from Satanic Bondage

1. Lord, break satanic chains in my life. Free me from darkness. In Jesus' name.

2. Heavenly Father, shatter satanic bondage. Release me into Your light. In Jesus' name.

3. Break every satanic hold. Liberate me, Lord. In Jesus' name.

4. Father, demolish satanic strongholds. Set me free. In Jesus' name.

5. Lord, break satanic chains. Release me from bondage. In Jesus' name.

6. Heavenly Father, dismantle every satanic grip. Grant me freedom. In Jesus' name.

7. Break the yoke of satanic oppression. Liberate me, Lord. In Jesus' name.

8. Father, release me from satanic bondage. Bring me into Your light. In Jesus' name.

9. Lord, break the power of Satan. Free me from darkness. In Jesus' name.

10. Heavenly Father, demolish satanic strongholds. Set me free. In Jesus' name.

11. Break every satanic chain. Liberate me, Lord. In Jesus' name.

12. Father, release me from satanic oppression. Bring me into Your light. In Jesus' name.

13. Lord, break the power of darkness. Free me from satanic bondage. In Jesus' name.

14. Heavenly Father, dismantle every satanic grip. Grant me freedom. In Jesus' name.

15. Break every satanic hold. Liberate me, Lord. In Jesus' name.

7.3. Prayer Against Placenta Bondage

1. Lord, break placenta bondage in my life. Free me from hidden chains. In Jesus' name.

2. Heavenly Father, shatter placenta bondage. Release me into Your freedom. In Jesus' name.

3. Break every placenta hold. Liberate me, Lord. In Jesus' name.

4. Father, demolish placenta strongholds. Set me free. In Jesus' name.

5. Lord, break placenta chains. Release me from hidden bondage. In Jesus' name.

6. Heavenly Father, dismantle every placenta grip. Grant me freedom. In Jesus' name.

7. Break the yoke of placenta oppression. Liberate me, Lord. In Jesus' name.

8. Father, release me from placenta bondage. Bring me into Your freedom. In Jesus' name.

9. Lord, break the power of placenta. Free me from hidden chains. In Jesus' name.

10. Heavenly Father, demolish placenta strongholds. Set me free. In Jesus' name.

11. Break every placenta chain. Liberate me, Lord. In Jesus' name.

12. Father, release me from placenta oppression. Bring me into Your freedom. In Jesus' name.

13. Lord, break the power of hidden bondage. Free me from placenta chains. In Jesus' name.

14. Heavenly Father, dismantle every placenta grip. Grant me freedom. In Jesus' name.

15. Break every placenta hold. Liberate me, Lord. In Jesus' name.

7.4. Prayer Against Foundational Bondage

1. Lord, break foundational bondage in my life. Free me from ancestral chains. In Jesus' name.

2. Heavenly Father, shatter foundational bondage. Release me into Your freedom. In Jesus' name.

3. Break every ancestral hold. Liberate me, Lord. In Jesus' name.

4. Father, demolish foundational strongholds. Set me free. In Jesus' name.

5. Lord, break foundational chains. Release me from ancestral bondage. In Jesus' name.

6. Heavenly Father, dismantle every foundational grip. Grant me freedom. In Jesus' name.

7. Break the yoke of ancestral oppression. Liberate me, Lord. In Jesus' name.

8. Father, release me from foundational bondage. Bring me into Your freedom. In Jesus' name.

9. Lord, break the power of foundations. Free me from ancestral chains. In Jesus' name.

10. Heavenly Father, demolish foundational strongholds. Set me free. In Jesus' name.

11. Break every foundational chain. Liberate me, Lord. In Jesus' name.

12. Father, release me from ancestral oppression. Bring me into Your freedom. In Jesus' name.

13. Lord, break the power of hidden bondage. Free me from foundational chains. In Jesus' name.

14. Heavenly Father, dismantle every foundational grip. Grant me freedom. In Jesus' name.

15. Break every foundational hold. Liberate me, Lord. In Jesus' name.

7.5. Prayer Against Bondage and Slavery

1. Lord, break the chains of bondage and slavery in my life. Liberate me, Father. In Jesus' name.

2. Heavenly Father, shatter the bonds of bondage and slavery. Grant me freedom, Lord. In Jesus' name.

3. Break every yoke of bondage and slavery. Liberate me, Father. In Jesus' name.

4. Father, demolish the strongholds of bondage and slavery. Set me free, Lord. In Jesus' name.

5. Lord, break the chains of bondage and slavery. Release me into Your freedom. In Jesus' name.

6. Heavenly Father, dismantle every grip of bondage and slavery. Grant me freedom, Lord. In Jesus' name.

7. Break the yoke of oppression and slavery. Liberate me, Father. In Jesus' name.

8. Father, release me from the shackles of bondage and slavery. Bring me into Your freedom. In Jesus' name.

9. Lord, break the power of bondage and slavery. Free me from every chain. In Jesus' name.

10. Heavenly Father, demolish the strongholds of bondage and slavery. Set me free, Lord. In Jesus' name.

11. Break every chain of bondage and slavery. Liberate me, Father. In Jesus' name.

12. Father, release me from the oppression of bondage and slavery. Bring me into Your freedom. In Jesus' name.

13. Lord, break the power of hidden bondage. Free me from the chains of slavery. In Jesus' name.

14. Heavenly Father, dismantle every grip of bondage and slavery. Grant me freedom, Lord. In Jesus' name.

15. Break every bond of slavery and oppression. Liberate me, Father. In Jesus' name.

7.6. Prayer to Break Stubborn Bondage

1. Lord, break stubborn bondage in my life. Liberate me from unyielding chains. In Jesus' name.

2. Heavenly Father, shatter the stronghold of stubborn bondage. Grant me freedom, Lord. In Jesus' name.

3. Break every unyielding yoke. Liberate me, Father. In Jesus' name.

4. Father, demolish the stubborn strongholds. Set me free from persistent chains. In Jesus' name.

5. Lord, break stubborn chains that resist release. Release me into Your freedom. In Jesus' name.

6. Heavenly Father, dismantle every grip of stubborn bondage. Grant me freedom, Lord. In Jesus' name.

7. Break the yoke of unyielding oppression. Liberate me from stubborn chains. In Jesus' name.

8. Father, release me from the shackles of stubborn bondage. Bring me into Your freedom. In Jesus' name.

9. Lord, break the power of stubborn chains. Free me from every persistent restraint. In Jesus' name.

10. Heavenly Father, demolish the stubborn strongholds. Set me free, Lord. In Jesus' name.

11. Break every stubborn chain that resists release. Liberate me, Father. In Jesus' name.

12. Father, release me from the oppression of stubborn bondage. Bring me into Your freedom. In Jesus' name.

13. Lord, break the power of hidden stubbornness. Free me from the chains of persistence. In Jesus' name.

14. Heavenly Father, dismantle every grip of stubborn bondage. Grant me freedom, Lord. In Jesus' name.

15. Break every bond of stubbornness and oppression. Liberate me, Father. In Jesus' name.

7.7. Breaking Evil Covenants

1. Lord, break evil covenants in my life. Annul every pact with darkness. In Jesus' name.

2. Heavenly Father, shatter the chains of evil covenants. Grant me freedom, Lord. In Jesus' name.

3. Break every unholy covenant. Liberate me, Father. In Jesus' name.

4. Father, demolish the sinister covenants. Set me free from unholy ties. In Jesus' name.

5. Lord, break the bonds of evil covenants. Release me into Your freedom. In Jesus' name.

6. Heavenly Father, dismantle every grip of evil covenants. Grant me freedom, Lord. In Jesus' name.

7. Break the yoke of dark covenants. Liberate me, Father. In Jesus' name.

8. Father, release me from the shackles of evil covenants. Bring me into Your freedom. In Jesus' name.

9. Lord, break the power of demonic covenants. Free me from every unholy pact. In Jesus' name.

10. Heavenly Father, demolish the sinister agreements. Set me free, Lord. In Jesus' name.

11. Break every covenant with darkness. Liberate me, Father. In Jesus' name.

12. Father, release me from the oppression of evil covenants. Bring me into Your freedom. In Jesus' name.

13. Lord, break the power of hidden darkness. Free me from the chains of unholy ties. In Jesus' name.

14. Heavenly Father, dismantle every grip of evil covenants. Grant me freedom, Lord. In Jesus' name.

15. Break every bond of dark agreements. Liberate me, Father. In Jesus' name.

Chapter 8

Prayer Against Poverty, Hardship & Reproach

All these blessings will come on you and accompany you if you obey the Lord your God... The Lord will open the heavens, the storehouse of his bounty, to send rain on your land in season and to bless all the work of your hands. You will lend to many nations but will borrow from none.

Deuteronomy 28:2, 12 (NIV)

8.1. Prayer to Eradicate Hardship

1. Lord, eradicate hardship in my life. Remove every burden. In Jesus' name.

2. Heavenly Father, shatter the chains of hardship. Bring ease, Lord. In Jesus' name.

3. Break every cycle of hardship. Liberate me, Father. In Jesus' name.

4. Father, demolish the stronghold of hardship. Bring relief from every struggle. In Jesus' name.

5. Lord, eradicate the bonds of hardship. Release me into Your ease. In Jesus' name.

6. Heavenly Father, dismantle every grip of hardship. Grant me comfort, Lord. In Jesus' name.

7. Break the yoke of enduring hardship. Liberate me, Father. In Jesus' name.

8. Father, release me from the shackles of hardship. Bring me into Your ease. In Jesus' name.

9. Lord, break the power of persistent hardship. Free me from every burden. In Jesus' name.

10. Heavenly Father, demolish the stronghold of difficulties. Bring relief, Lord. In Jesus' name.

11. Break every cycle of enduring hardship. Liberate me, Father. In Jesus' name.

12. Father, release me from the oppression of relentless hardship. Bring me into Your ease. In Jesus' name.

13. Lord, break the power of hidden struggles. Free me from the chains of hardship. In Jesus' name.

14. Heavenly Father, dismantle every grip of persistent difficulty. Grant me comfort, Lord. In Jesus' name.

15. Break every bond of enduring hardship. Liberate me, Father. In Jesus' name.

8.2. Prayer to Remove Evil Limitations

1. Lord, remove evil limitations in my life. Break every restricting barrier. In Jesus' name.

2. Heavenly Father, shatter the chains of evil limitations. Grant me boundless freedom, Lord. In Jesus' name.

3. Break every restricting limit. Liberate me, Father. In Jesus' name.

4. Father, demolish the stronghold of evil limitations. Set me free from every hindrance. In Jesus' name.

5. Lord, remove the bonds of restrictive limits. Release me into Your expansive grace. In Jesus' name.

6. Heavenly Father, dismantle every grip of evil limitations. Grant me limitless possibilities, Lord. In Jesus' name.

7. Break the yoke of limiting oppression. Liberate me, Father. In Jesus' name.

8. Father, release me from the shackles of evil limitations. Bring me into Your boundless favor. In Jesus' name.

9. Lord, break the power of constricting limits. Free me from every hindering constraint. In Jesus' name.

10. Heavenly Father, demolish the stronghold of restricting limitations. Set me free, Lord. In Jesus' name.

11. Break every limiting chain. Liberate me, Father. In Jesus' name.

12. Father, release me from the oppression of evil limitations. Bring me into Your expansive grace. In Jesus' name.

13. Lord, break the power of hidden constraints. Free me from the chains of limitations. In Jesus' name.

14. Heavenly Father, dismantle every grip of constricting limitations. Grant me limitless possibilities, Lord. In Jesus' name.

15. Break every bond of restricting oppression. Liberate me, Father. In Jesus' name.

8.3. Prayer Against the Marks of Hatred and Rejection

1. Lord, erase the marks of hatred and rejection from my life. Remove every hurtful imprint. In Jesus' name.

2. Heavenly Father, wash away the scars of hatred and rejection. Flood my heart with Your love, Lord. In Jesus' name.

3. Break every lingering mark of hatred. Liberate me, Father. In Jesus' name.

4. Father, demolish the stronghold of rejection's marks. Set me free from every painful reminder. In Jesus' name.

5. Lord, remove the stains of hatred and rejection. Let Your acceptance be my covering. In Jesus' name.

6. Heavenly Father, dismantle every grip of hurtful marks. Fill me with Your healing, Lord. In Jesus' name.

7. Break the yoke of lingering pain. Liberate me, Father. In Jesus' name.

8. Father, release me from the shackles of hatred's marks. Wrap me in the warmth of Your acceptance. In Jesus' name.

9. Lord, break the power of persistent marks of rejection. Free me from every haunting memory. In Jesus' name.

10. Heavenly Father, demolish the stronghold of hurtful reminders. Set me free, Lord. In Jesus' name.

11. Erase every mark of lingering hatred. Liberate me, Father. In Jesus' name.

12. Father, release me from the oppression of rejection's marks. Cover me with Your healing grace. In Jesus' name.

13. Lord, break the power of hidden wounds. Free me from the chains of rejection's marks. In Jesus' name.

14. Heavenly Father, dismantle every grip of lingering pain. Fill me with Your soothing balm, Lord. In Jesus' name.

15. Break every bond of hurtful reminders. Liberate me, Father. In Jesus' name.

8.4. Prayer to Overpower Household Wickedness

1. Lord, empower me to overcome household wickedness. Let Your light dispel every darkness. In Jesus' name.

2. Heavenly Father, grant me strength to overpower the wickedness within my home. Bring Your peace, Lord. In Jesus' name.

3. Break the hold of household wickedness. Liberate me, Father. In Jesus' name.

4. Father, demolish the stronghold of darkness within my household. Set us free, Lord. In Jesus' name.

5. Lord, empower me to conquer the wicked forces within my home. Let Your love reign, In Jesus' name.

6. Heavenly Father, dismantle every grip of household wickedness. Bring Your divine order, Lord. In Jesus' name.

7. Break the yoke of malevolent oppression. Liberate my home, Father. In Jesus' name.

8. Father, release us from the shackles of household wickedness. Bring divine harmony, Lord. In Jesus' name.

9. Lord, break the power of persistent wickedness within my home. Free us from every evil influence. In Jesus' name.

10. Heavenly Father, demolish the stronghold of darkness. Set us free, Lord. In Jesus' name.

11. Empower me to uproot every wicked force within my home. Let Your light shine brightly, Lord. In Jesus' name.

12. Father, release us from the oppression of household wickedness. Bring Your divine order, Lord. In Jesus' name.

13. Lord, break the power of hidden malevolence. Free us from the chains of wickedness. In Jesus' name.

14. Heavenly Father, dismantle every grip of oppressive forces. Bring Your divine peace, Lord. In Jesus' name.

15. Break every bond of household wickedness. Liberate my home, Father. In Jesus' name.

8.5. Stepping Out of the Tail Region (Backwardness)

1. Lord, guide my steps out of the tail region of backwardness. Lead me forward, Father. In Jesus' name.

2. Heavenly Father, lift me from the hindmost places of backwardness. Propel me towards progress, Lord. In Jesus' name.

3. Break the chains of tail region backwardness. Liberate me, Father. In Jesus' name.

4. Father, demolish the stronghold of lagging behind. Set me on the path of advancement, Lord. In Jesus' name.

5. Lord, lead me out of the shadows of backwardness. Let Your light guide my way. In Jesus' name.

6. Heavenly Father, dismantle every grip of hindering forces. Propel me forward, Lord. In Jesus' name.

7. Break the yoke of trailing behind. Liberate me from stagnation, Father. In Jesus' name.

8. Father, release me from the shackles of tail region backwardness. Set my feet on the path of progress. In Jesus' name.

9. Lord, break the power of persistent backwardness. Free me from every dragging force. In Jesus' name.

10. Heavenly Father, demolish the stronghold of lagging. Propel me forward, Lord. In Jesus' name.

11. Guide me out of the lingering shadows of backwardness. Let Your light illuminate my path, Lord. In Jesus' name.

12. Father, release me from the oppression of being behind. Set me on the track of advancement. In Jesus' name.

13. Lord, break the power of hidden forces pulling me backward. Free me from every hindrance. In Jesus' name.

14. Heavenly Father, dismantle every grip of hindering influences. Propel me forward, Lord. In Jesus' name.

15. Break every bond of tail region backwardness. Liberate me, Father. In Jesus' name.

8.6. Prayer to Overcome Reproach and Shame

1. Lord, empower me to overcome reproach and shame. Clothe me in Your dignity. In Jesus' name.

2. Heavenly Father, lift me from the depths of reproach and shame. Cover me with Your grace, Lord. In Jesus' name.

3. Break the chains of reproach and shame. Liberate me, Father. In Jesus' name.

4. Father, demolish the stronghold of disgrace. Surround me with Your honor, Lord. In Jesus' name.

5. Lord, lead me out of the shadows of reproach. Let Your light dispel every shame. In Jesus' name.

6. Heavenly Father, dismantle every grip of humiliating forces. Envelop me in Your glory, Lord. In Jesus' name.

7. Break the yoke of demeaning oppression. Liberate me, Father. In Jesus' name.

8. Father, release me from the shackles of reproach and shame. Clothe me in Your righteousness, Lord. In Jesus' name.

9. Lord, break the power of persistent disgrace. Free me from every condemning voice. In Jesus' name.

10. Heavenly Father, demolish the stronghold of shame. Surround me with Your favor, Lord. In Jesus' name.

11. Guide me out of the lingering shadows of reproach. Let Your light illuminate my path, Lord. In Jesus' name.

12. Father, release me from the oppression of shame. Clothe me in Your acceptance, Lord. In Jesus' name.

13. Lord, break the power of hidden forces causing reproach. Free me from every condemning influence. In Jesus' name.

14. Heavenly Father, dismantle every grip of humiliating oppression. Envelop me in Your glory, Lord. In Jesus' name.

15. Break every bond of reproach and shame. Liberate me, Father. In Jesus' name.

8.7. Prayer to Transition from Poverty to Prosperity

1. Lord, guide my journey from poverty to prosperity. Open doors of abundance, Father. In Jesus' name.

2. Heavenly Father, lead me out of the grip of lack and scarcity. Shower me with prosperity, Lord. In Jesus' name.

3. Break the chains of poverty. Liberate me, Father. In Jesus' name.

4. Father, demolish the stronghold of financial struggle. Set me on the path of prosperity, Lord. In Jesus' name.

5. Lord, transition me from the shadows of poverty. Let Your wealth and abundance overflow. In Jesus' name.

6. Heavenly Father, dismantle every grip of limiting forces. Propel me forward into prosperity, Lord. In Jesus' name.

7. Break the yoke of financial oppression. Liberate me, Father. In Jesus' name.

8. Father, release me from the shackles of poverty. Bring me into Your prosperity and abundance, Lord. In Jesus' name.

9. Lord, break the power of persistent financial struggle. Free me from every hindrance to prosperity. In Jesus' name.

10. Heavenly Father, demolish the stronghold of lack. Set me on the track of financial prosperity, Lord. In Jesus' name.

11. Guide me out of the lingering shadows of poverty. Let Your light illuminate my financial path, Lord. In Jesus' name.

12. Father, release me from the oppression of financial lack. Clothe me in the garment of Your prosperity, Lord. In Jesus' name.

13. Lord, break the power of hidden forces causing poverty. Free me from every financial limitation. In Jesus' name.

14. Heavenly Father, dismantle every grip of restricting influences. Propel me forward into financial prosperity, Lord. In Jesus' name.

15. Break every bond of poverty. Liberate me, Father. In Jesus' name.

Chapter 9

Prayer Against Demonic Yokes

Come to me, all you who are weary and burdened, and I will give you rest. Take my yoke upon you and learn from me, for I am gentle and humble in heart, and you will find rest for your souls. For my yoke is easy and my burden is light.

Matthew 11:28-30 (NIV)

9.1. Prayer to Break the Yoke of Sexual Demons

1. Lord, break the yoke of sexual demons in my life. Release me from their grip, Father. In Jesus' name.

2. Heavenly Father, shatter the chains of sexual bondage. Liberate me, Lord. In Jesus' name.

3. Break the yoke of sexual oppression. Free me from every demonic influence, Father. In Jesus' name.

4. Father, demolish the stronghold of sexual demons. Set me free from their captivity, Lord. In Jesus' name.

5. Lord, lead me out of the shadows of sexual bondage. Let Your purity and holiness reign, Father. In Jesus' name.

6. Heavenly Father, dismantle every grip of impure forces. Cleanse and sanctify me, Lord. In Jesus' name.

7. Break the chains of demonic interference. Liberate me, Father. In Jesus' name.

8. Father, release me from the shackles of sexual demons. Cleanse me with Your redeeming power, Lord. In Jesus' name.

9. Lord, break the power of persistent sexual struggles. Free me from every unholy influence, Father. In Jesus' name.

10. Heavenly Father, demolish the stronghold of impurity. Set me on the path of sexual purity, Lord. In Jesus' name.

11. Guide me out of the lingering shadows of sexual bondage. Let Your light shine brightly, Father. In Jesus' name.

12. Father, release me from the oppression of sexual demons. Purify and sanctify me, Lord. In Jesus' name.

13. Lord, break the power of hidden forces causing sexual bondage. Free me from every demonic interference, Father. In Jesus' name.

14. Heavenly Father, dismantle every grip of impure influences. Set me free, Lord. In Jesus' name.

15. Break every bond of sexual demons. Liberate me, Father. In Jesus' name.

9.2. Prayer to Eliminate the Yoke of Ignorance

1. Lord, eliminate the yoke of ignorance from my life. Illuminate my mind with Your wisdom, Father. In Jesus' name.

2. Heavenly Father, break the chains of ignorance that bind my understanding. Enlighten me, Lord. In Jesus' name.

3. Break the yoke of mental oppression. Liberate my mind from the darkness of ignorance, Father. In Jesus' name.

4. Father, demolish the stronghold of ignorance that clouds my judgment. Set me free, Lord. In Jesus' name.

5. Lord, lead me out of the shadows of ignorance. Let Your knowledge and insight guide my path, Father. In Jesus' name.

6. Heavenly Father, dismantle every grip of limiting forces. Open my mind to Your understanding, Lord. In Jesus' name.

7. Break the chains of mental bondage. Liberate me, Father. In Jesus' name.

8. Father, release me from the shackles of ignorance. Fill my mind with Your divine wisdom, Lord. In Jesus' name.

9. Lord, break the power of persistent mental struggles. Free me from every hindrance to understanding, Father. In Jesus' name.

10. Heavenly Father, demolish the stronghold of mental darkness. Set me on the path of knowledge and discernment, Lord. In Jesus' name.

11. Guide me out of the lingering shadows of ignorance. Let Your light shine brightly, Father. In Jesus' name.

12. Father, release me from the oppression of ignorance. Fill my mind with Your divine revelation, Lord. In Jesus' name.

13. Lord, break the power of hidden forces causing mental bondage. Free me from every limiting thought, Father. In Jesus' name.

14. Heavenly Father, dismantle every grip of mental obscurity. Set me free, Lord. In Jesus' name.

15. Break every bond of ignorance. Liberate my mind, Father. In Jesus' name.

9.3. Prayer Against the Yokes of Hell

1. Heavenly Father, I come before You to break the yokes of hell in my life. Release me from every demonic bondage, Lord. In Jesus' name.

2. Lord, shatter the chains of darkness that seek to bind me. Liberate me from the yokes of hell, Father. In Jesus' name.

3. Break the yoke of infernal oppression. Free me from every demonic influence, Father. In Jesus' name.

4. Father, demolish the stronghold of hellish forces. Set me free from their grip, Lord. In Jesus' name.

5. Lord, lead me out of the shadows of demonic bondage. Let Your light dispel every darkness, Father. In Jesus' name.

6. Heavenly Father, dismantle every grip of malevolent forces. Cleanse and purify me, Lord. In Jesus' name.

7. Break the chains of demonic interference. Liberate me from the yokes of hell, Father. In Jesus' name.

8. Father, release me from the shackles of satanic oppression. Cover me with Your protective armor, Lord. In Jesus' name.

9. Lord, break the power of persistent demonic struggles. Free me from every unholy influence, Father. In Jesus' name.

10. Heavenly Father, demolish the stronghold of darkness. Set me on the path of righteousness, Lord. In Jesus' name.

11. Guide me out of the lingering shadows of demonic bondage. Let Your light shine brightly, Father. In Jesus' name.

12. Father, release me from the oppression of hellish forces. Purify and sanctify me, Lord. In Jesus' name.

13. Lord, break the power of hidden forces causing demonic bondage. Free me from every satanic interference, Father. In Jesus' name.

14. Heavenly Father, dismantle every grip of malevolent influences. Set me free, Lord. In Jesus' name.

15. Break every bond of hellish yokes. Liberate me from the clutches of darkness, Father. In Jesus' name.

Chapter 10

Prayer To Overpower Witchcraft

Whoever dwells in the shelter of the Most High will rest in the shadow of the Almighty. I will say of the Lord, 'He is my refuge and my fortress, my God, in whom I trust.' Surely he will save you from the fowler's snare and from the deadly pestilence.

Psalm 91:1-3 (NIV)

10.1. Prayer for Protection Against Witchcraft Powers

1. Heavenly Father, I come before You seeking protection against witchcraft powers. Shield me with Your divine armor, Lord. In Jesus' name.

2. Lord, break the influence of every witchcraft power seeking to harm me. Cover me with Your protective wings, Father. In Jesus' name.

3. Break the yoke of malevolent witchcraft forces. Liberate me from every dark spell, Father. In Jesus' name.

4. Father, demolish the stronghold of witchcraft that seeks to bind me. Set me free from their influence, Lord. In Jesus' name.

5. Lord, lead me out of the shadows of witchcraft. Let Your light dispel every dark enchantment, Father. In Jesus' name.

6. Heavenly Father, dismantle every grip of nefarious forces. Cleanse and purify me from every curse, Lord. In Jesus' name.

7. Break the chains of demonic interference. Liberate me from the influence of witchcraft powers, Father. In Jesus' name.

8. Father, release me from the shackles of dark enchantments. Cover me with Your protective shield, Lord. In Jesus' name.

9. Lord, break the power of persistent witchcraft struggles. Free me from every unholy influence, Father. In Jesus' name.

10. Heavenly Father, demolish the stronghold of dark spells. Set me on the path of righteousness, Lord. In Jesus' name.

11. Guide me out of the lingering shadows of witchcraft. Let Your light shine brightly, Father. In Jesus' name.

12. Father, release me from the oppression of witchcraft powers. Purify and sanctify me, Lord. In Jesus' name.

13. Lord, break the power of hidden forces causing witchcraft influence. Free me from every malevolent interference, Father. In Jesus' name.

14. Heavenly Father, dismantle every grip of evil influences. Set me free, Lord. In Jesus' name.

15. Break every bond of witchcraft powers. Liberate me from their dark schemes, Father. In Jesus' name.

16. Lord, nullify every evil potion and charm crafted against me by witchcraft. Let their schemes be rendered powerless, Father. In Jesus' name.

17. Break the hold of every cursed object associated with witchcraft. Release me from their malevolent influence, Lord. In Jesus' name.

18. Heavenly Father, expose and thwart every hidden agenda of witchcraft powers operating against me. Let their plans crumble, Father. In Jesus' name.

19. Father, I declare that no weapon formed through witchcraft against me shall prosper. Let every tongue that rises against me be silenced, Lord. In Jesus' name.

20. Lord, fortify my spiritual defenses against the attacks of witchcraft. Clothe me in the full armor of God, Father. In Jesus' name.

21. Father, I release Your consuming fire upon every witchcraft altar and coven working against me. Let their powers be utterly destroyed, Lord. In Jesus' name.

10.2. Prayer to Defend Against Witchcraft Attacks

1. Lord, shield me from witchcraft plots. No weapon formed shall prosper against me. In Jesus' name.

2. Break every spell cast. I declare divine protection. In Jesus' name.

3. Nullify evil enchantments. I stand covered in Your armor. In Jesus' name.

4. Lord, expose hidden curses. Your light dispels dark schemes. In Jesus' name.

5. Break demonic influence. Set me free from their grip. In Jesus' name.

6. Guard me against hexes. Your power prevails over darkness. In Jesus' name.

7. Dismantle every grip of darkness. Cleanse and purify me. In Jesus' name.

8. Break chains of interference. Liberate me from evil spells. In Jesus' name.

9. Release me from oppression. Cover me with Your shield. In Jesus' name.

10. Break persistent struggles. Free me from unholy influence. In Jesus' name.

11. Demolish dark strongholds. Set me on righteousness's path. In Jesus' name.

12. Guide me from lingering shadows. Let Your light shine. In Jesus' name.

13. Release me from wicked oppression. Purify and sanctify me. In Jesus' name.

14. Break hidden forces. Free me from malevolent interference. In Jesus' name.

15. Dismantle unholy influences. Set me free, Lord. In Jesus' name.

10.3. Prayer to Annihilate Witchcraft Powers

1. Heavenly Father, annihilate every witchcraft power working against my life. Let Your consuming fire destroy their influence, Lord. In Jesus' name.

2. Lord, expose and obliterate every hidden agenda of witchcraft powers. Let their plans crumble into dust, Father. In Jesus' name.

3. Break the yoke of every demonic spell cast by witchcraft. Liberate me from their grip, Father. In Jesus' name.

4. Father, demolish the stronghold of malevolent witchcraft powers. Set me free from their bondage, Lord. In Jesus' name.

5. Lord, lead me out of the shadows of unholy enchantments. Let Your light dispel every dark influence, Father. In Jesus' name.

6. Heavenly Father, dismantle every grip of malevolent forces tied to witchcraft. Cleanse and purify me, Lord. In Jesus' name.

7. Break the chains of demonic interference. Liberate me from the influence of evil witchcraft powers, Father. In Jesus' name.

8. Father, release me from the shackles of unholy spiritual manipulations. Cover me with Your divine protection, Lord. In Jesus' name.

9. Lord, break the power of persistent struggles connected to witchcraft. Free me from every unholy influence, Father. In Jesus' name.

10. Heavenly Father, demolish the stronghold of dark spiritual forces. Set me on the path of righteousness, Lord. In Jesus' name.

11. Guide me out of the lingering shadows of malevolent witchcraft powers. Let Your light shine brightly, Father. In Jesus' name.

12. Father, release me from the oppression of wicked spiritual forces. Purify and sanctify me, Lord. In Jesus' name.

13. Lord, break the power of hidden forces connected to malevolent witchcraft. Free me from every malevolent interference, Father. In Jesus' name.

14. Heavenly Father, dismantle every grip of unholy influences. Set me free, Lord. In Jesus' name.

15. Break every bond of malevolent witchcraft powers. Liberate me from their dark schemes, Father. In Jesus' name.

Chapter 11

Prayer Against Evil Altars

For our struggle is not against flesh and blood, but against the rulers, against the authorities, against the powers of this dark world and against the spiritual forces of evil in the heavenly realms.

Ephesians 6:12 (NIV)

11.1. Prayer for Breaking Evil Covenants

1. Heavenly Father, I come before You to break every evil covenant that may be affecting my life. Nullify their influence, Lord. In Jesus' name.

2. Lord, break every unholy covenant that I might have entered knowingly or unknowingly. Release me from their grip, Father. In Jesus' name.

3. Break the yoke of every covenant made with darkness. Liberate me from their influence, Father. In Jesus' name.

4. Father, demolish the stronghold of evil covenants that may be operating in my life. Set me free from their bondage, Lord. In Jesus' name.

5. Lord, lead me out of the shadows of unholy covenants. Let Your light dispel every dark agreement, Father. In Jesus' name.

6. Heavenly Father, dismantle every grip of malevolent forces tied to evil covenants. Cleanse and purify me, Lord. In Jesus' name.

7. Break the chains of demonic interference. Liberate me from the influence of evil covenants, Father. In Jesus' name.

8. Father, release me from the shackles of unholy agreements. Cover me with Your redeeming power, Lord. In Jesus' name.

9. Lord, break the power of persistent struggles connected to evil covenants. Free me from every unholy influence, Father. In Jesus' name.

10. Heavenly Father, demolish the stronghold of dark pacts. Set me on the path of righteousness, Lord. In Jesus' name.

11. Guide me out of the lingering shadows of evil covenants. Let Your light shine brightly, Father. In Jesus' name.

12. Father, release me from the oppression of wicked agreements. Purify and sanctify me, Lord. In Jesus' name.

13. Lord, break the power of hidden forces tied to evil covenants. Free me from every malevolent interference, Father. In Jesus' name.

14. Heavenly Father, dismantle every grip of unholy influences. Set me free, Lord. In Jesus' name.

15. Break every bond of evil covenants. Liberate me from their dark schemes, Father. In Jesus' name.

11.2. Prayer Against Malevolent Altars

1. Heavenly Father, I come before You to break the power of every malevolent altar operating against my life. Consume them with Your holy fire, Lord. In Jesus' name.

2. Lord, expose and dismantle every wicked altar set up against me. Let their influence be utterly destroyed, Father. In Jesus' name.

3. Break the yoke of every demonic altar erected to harm me. Liberate me from their grip, Father. In Jesus' name.

4. Father, demolish the stronghold of malevolent altars that may be influencing my life. Set me free from their bondage, Lord. In Jesus' name.

5. Lord, lead me out of the shadows of unholy altars. Let Your light dispel every dark influence, Father. In Jesus' name.

6. Heavenly Father, dismantle every grip of malevolent forces connected to wicked altars. Cleanse and purify me, Lord. In Jesus' name.

7. Break the chains of demonic interference. Liberate me from the influence of malevolent altars, Father. In Jesus' name.

8. Father, release me from the shackles of unholy spiritual platforms. Cover me with Your divine protection, Lord. In Jesus' name.

9. Lord, break the power of persistent struggles tied to malevolent altars. Free me from every unholy influence, Father. In Jesus' name.

10. Heavenly Father, demolish the stronghold of dark spiritual structures. Set me on the path of righteousness, Lord. In Jesus' name.

11. Guide me out of the lingering shadows of malevolent altars. Let Your light shine brightly, Father. In Jesus' name.

12. Father, release me from the oppression of wicked spiritual platforms. Purify and sanctify me, Lord. In Jesus' name.

13. Lord, break the power of hidden forces connected to malevolent altars. Free me from every malevolent interference, Father. In Jesus' name.

14. Heavenly Father, dismantle every grip of unholy influences. Set me free, Lord. In Jesus' name.

15. Break every bond of malevolent altars. Liberate me from their dark schemes, Father. In Jesus' name.

11.3. Prayer to Paralyze Evil Sacrifices

1. Heavenly Father, I come before You, seeking protection from every evil sacrifice plotted against me. Paralyze and nullify their power, Lord. In Jesus' name.

2. Lord, expose and thwart every hidden agenda of evil sacrifices targeted at my life. Let their plans crumble, Father. In Jesus' name.

3. Break the yoke of every demonic sacrifice made to harm me. Liberate me from their grip, Father. In Jesus' name.

4. Father, demolish the stronghold of malevolent sacrifices that may be operating against me. Set me free from their bondage, Lord. In Jesus' name.

5. Lord, lead me out of the shadows of unholy sacrifices. Let Your light dispel every dark ritual, Father. In Jesus' name.

6. Heavenly Father, dismantle every grip of malevolent forces connected to wicked sacrifices. Cleanse and purify me, Lord. In Jesus' name.

7. Break the chains of demonic interference. Liberate me from the influence of evil sacrifices, Father. In Jesus' name.

8. Father, release me from the shackles of unholy spiritual offerings. Cover me with Your divine protection, Lord. In Jesus' name.

9. Lord, break the power of persistent struggles tied to malevolent sacrifices. Free me from every unholy influence, Father. In Jesus' name.

10. Heavenly Father, demolish the stronghold of dark spiritual rituals. Set me on the path of righteousness, Lord. In Jesus' name.

11. Guide me out of the lingering shadows of evil sacrifices. Let Your light shine brightly, Father. In Jesus' name.

12. Father, release me from the oppression of wicked spiritual offerings. Purify and sanctify me, Lord. In Jesus' name.

13. Lord, break the power of hidden forces connected to malevolent sacrifices. Free me from every malevolent interference, Father. In Jesus' name.

14. Heavenly Father, dismantle every grip of unholy influences. Set me free, Lord. In Jesus' name.

15. Break every bond of malevolent sacrifices. Liberate me from their dark schemes, Father. In Jesus' name.

Chapter 12

Prayer Against All Manner Of Curses

The Lord will grant that the enemies who rise up against you will be defeated before you. They will come at you from one direction but flee from you in seven."

Deuteronomy 28:7 (NIV)

12.1. Prayer to Overcome Destructive Curses

1. Heavenly Father, empower me to overcome every destructive curse placed upon my life. Let Your blessing override every curse, Lord. In Jesus' name.

2. Lord, expose and break every hidden curse that may be operating against me. Let their power be shattered, Father. In Jesus' name.

3. Break the yoke of every destructive curse spoken over my life. Liberate me from their grip, Father. In Jesus' name.

4. Father, demolish the stronghold of malevolent curses. Set me free from their bondage, Lord. In Jesus' name.

5. Lord, lead me out of the shadows of unholy maledictions. Let Your light dispel every dark influence, Father. In Jesus' name.

6. Heavenly Father, dismantle every grip of malevolent forces tied to curses. Cleanse and purify me, Lord. In Jesus' name.

7. Break the chains of demonic interference. Liberate me from the influence of destructive curses, Father. In Jesus' name.

8. Father, release me from the shackles of unholy spiritual condemnations. Cover me with Your divine protection, Lord. In Jesus' name.

9. Lord, break the power of persistent struggles connected to destructive curses. Free me from every unholy influence, Father. In Jesus' name.

10. Heavenly Father, demolish the stronghold of dark spiritual forces. Set me on the path of righteousness, Lord. In Jesus' name.

11. Guide me out of the lingering shadows of malevolent curses. Let Your light shine brightly, Father. In Jesus' name.

12. Father, release me from the oppression of wicked spiritual condemnations. Purify and sanctify me, Lord. In Jesus' name.

13. Lord, break the power of hidden forces connected to destructive curses. Free me from every malevolent interference, Father. In Jesus' name.

14. Heavenly Father, dismantle every grip of unholy influences. Set me free, Lord. In Jesus' name.

15. Break every bond of destructive curses. Liberate me from their dark schemes, Father. In Jesus' name.

12.2. Prayer to Terminate Hidden Curses

1. Heavenly Father, I come before You to terminate every hidden curse affecting my life. Let Your divine intervention nullify their power, Lord. In Jesus' name.

2. Lord, expose and terminate every concealed curse that may be operating against me. Let their influence be shattered, Father. In Jesus' name.

3. Break the yoke of every hidden curse silently spoken over my life. Liberate me from their grip, Father. In Jesus' name.

4. Father, demolish the stronghold of malevolent hidden curses. Set me free from their bondage, Lord. In Jesus' name.

5. Lord, lead me out of the shadows of unholy covert maledictions. Let Your light dispel every dark influence, Father. In Jesus' name.

6. Heavenly Father, dismantle every grip of malevolent forces tied to hidden curses. Cleanse and purify me, Lord. In Jesus' name.

7. Break the chains of demonic interference. Liberate me from the influence of hidden curses, Father. In Jesus' name.

8. Father, release me from the shackles of unholy spiritual condemnations. Cover me with Your divine protection, Lord. In Jesus' name.

9. Lord, break the power of persistent struggles connected to hidden curses. Free me from every unholy influence, Father. In Jesus' name.

10. Heavenly Father, demolish the stronghold of dark spiritual forces. Set me on the path of righteousness, Lord. In Jesus' name.

11. Guide me out of the lingering shadows of malevolent hidden curses. Let Your light shine brightly, Father. In Jesus' name.

12. Father, release me from the oppression of wicked spiritual condemnations. Purify and sanctify me, Lord. In Jesus' name.

13. Lord, break the power of hidden forces connected to destructive curses. Free me from every malevolent interference, Father. In Jesus' name.

14. Heavenly Father, dismantle every grip of unholy influences. Set me free, Lord. In Jesus' name.

15. Break every bond of hidden curses. Liberate me from their dark schemes, Father. In Jesus' name.

12.3. Prayer to Abolish Demonic Curses

1. Heavenly Father, I stand before You, seeking the abolition of every demonic curse afflicting my life. Let Your divine power shatter their influence, Lord. In Jesus' name.

2. Lord, expose and annihilate every demonic curse that may be operating against me. Let their dark influence be obliterated, Father. In Jesus' name.

3. Break the yoke of every demonic curse spoken against me. Liberate me from their grip, Father. In Jesus' name.

4. Father, demolish the stronghold of malevolent demonic curses. Set me free from their bondage, Lord. In Jesus' name.

5. Lord, lead me out of the shadows of unholy diabolic maledictions. Let Your divine light dispel every dark influence, Father. In Jesus' name.

6. Heavenly Father, dismantle every grip of malevolent demonic forces tied to curses. Cleanse and purify me, Lord. In Jesus' name.

7. Break the chains of demonic interference. Liberate me from the influence of diabolic curses, Father. In Jesus' name.

8. Father, release me from the shackles of unholy spiritual condemnations. Cover me with Your divine protection, Lord. In Jesus' name.

9. Lord, break the power of persistent struggles connected to demonic curses. Free me from every unholy influence, Father. In Jesus' name.

10. Heavenly Father, demolish the stronghold of dark demonic forces. Set me on the path of righteousness, Lord. In Jesus' name.

11. Guide me out of the lingering shadows of malevolent demonic curses. Let Your divine light shine brightly, Father. In Jesus' name.

12. Father, release me from the oppression of wicked demonic condemnations. Purify and sanctify me, Lord. In Jesus' name.

13. Lord, break the power of hidden forces connected to demonic curses. Free me from every malevolent interference, Father. In Jesus' name.

14. Heavenly Father, dismantle every grip of unholy influences. Set me free, Lord. In Jesus' name.

15. Break every bond of demonic curses. Liberate me from their dark schemes, Father. In Jesus' name.

Chapter 13

Prayer For Breakthroughs And Prosperity

For I know the plans I have for you, declares the Lord, plans for welfare and not for evil, to give you a future and a hope.

Jeremiah 29:11 (NIV):

Bring the whole tithe into the storehouse, that there may be food in my house. Test me in this," says the Lord Almighty, "and see if I will not throw open the floodgates of heaven and pour out so much blessing that there will not be room enough to store it.

Malachi 3:10 (NIV)

13.1. Prayer Against Financial Burdens

1. Heavenly Father, I lift my financial burdens to You. Provide for my needs according to Your riches in glory. In Jesus' name.

2. Lord, break the chains of financial stress. Let Your abundance flow into my life. In Jesus' name.

3. Father, I surrender my financial struggles to You. Open doors of prosperity and pour out blessings. In Jesus' name.

4. Break the cycle of lack, Lord. Let financial abundance overflow in my life. In Jesus' name.

5. Heavenly Father, release Your financial favor upon me. Let Your provision surpass all my needs. In Jesus' name.

6. Lord, dismantle the stronghold of financial burdens. Bring forth opportunities and increase, Father. In Jesus' name.

7. Break every financial limitation, Lord. Open the windows of heaven and pour out a blessing. In Jesus' name.

8. Father, release me from the shackles of debt. Let financial breakthroughs manifest in my life. In Jesus' name.

9. Lord, bless the work of my hands. Let prosperity and success be my portion. In Jesus' name.

10. Heavenly Father, I declare financial freedom. Let Your abundance overflow in my finances. In Jesus' name.

11. Break the cycle of financial hardship, Lord. Let Your financial grace abound in my life. In Jesus' name.

12. Father, I trust You with my financial worries. Provide a way where there seems to be no way. In Jesus' name.

13. Lord, open doors of financial breakthrough. Let Your favor shine upon my financial endeavors. In Jesus' name.

14. Break every financial barrier, Lord. Let Your prosperity reign in every area of my life. In Jesus' name.

15. Heavenly Father, I receive Your financial blessings with gratitude. Let Your abundance overflow in my finances. In Jesus' name.

13.2. Prayer for Divine Elevation

1. Heavenly Father, I lift my heart to You in prayer, seeking divine elevation in every area of my life. Lift me to new heights, Lord. In Jesus' name.

2. Lord, let Your divine favor elevate me in the eyes of those around me. Open doors of opportunity and advancement, Father. In Jesus' name.

3. Father, break every limitation hindering my elevation. Propel me to the heights You have destined for me. In Jesus' name.

4. Lord, dismantle every obstacle blocking my path to divine elevation. Let Your grace lift me beyond my wildest dreams, Father. In Jesus' name.

5. Heavenly Father, I surrender my ambitions to You. Elevate me according to Your perfect plan for my life. In Jesus' name.

6. Lord, I declare an end to mediocrity. Elevate me to places of influence and impact, Father. In Jesus' name.

7. Break every chain of stagnation, Lord. Elevate me to a level where Your glory shines brightly through my life. In Jesus' name.

8. Father, release divine wisdom and discernment as I navigate the path to elevation. Guide my steps, Lord. In Jesus' name.

9. Lord, let Your divine promotion distinguish me among my peers. Elevation comes from You alone, Father. In Jesus' name.

10. Heavenly Father, I trust in Your timing for my elevation. Let patience and perseverance mark my journey, Lord. In Jesus' name.

11. Break the cycle of limitations, Lord. Elevate me to a position of influence where I can make a positive impact. In Jesus' name.

12. Father, I surrender my ambitions to You. Elevate me to places where I can glorify Your name, Lord. In Jesus' name.

13. Lord, I declare an end to every setback. Elevate me to a realm of breakthroughs and accomplishments, Father. In Jesus' name.

14. Break every spirit of discouragement, Lord. Elevate my spirit and fill me with hope for the future. In Jesus' name.

15. Heavenly Father, as I seek divine elevation, let Your favor rest upon me. Lift me higher, Lord, for Your glory. In Jesus' name.

13.3. Prayer for Lasting Wealth

1. Heavenly Father, I come before You, seeking Your divine favor for lasting wealth. Bless the work of my hands, Lord, and grant me enduring prosperity. In Jesus' name.

2. Lord, break every cycle of financial struggle. Open doors of abundance and provide lasting wealth, Father. In Jesus' name.

3. Father, I surrender my financial endeavors to You. Establish me in lasting wealth that glorifies Your name. In Jesus' name.

4. Break every chain of financial instability, Lord. Let lasting wealth flow into every area of my life, Father. In Jesus' name.

5. Heavenly Father, release Your financial favor upon me. Let lasting wealth be my portion, and may I be a blessing to others. In Jesus' name.

6. Lord, dismantle the stronghold of lack. Establish me in lasting wealth that testifies to Your faithfulness, Father. In Jesus' name.

7. Break every financial limitation, Lord. Let lasting wealth be a testimony to Your provision and grace, Father. In Jesus' name.

8. Father, release me from the shackles of debt. Let lasting wealth and financial freedom be my inheritance. In Jesus' name.

9. Lord, bless the work of my hands. Let prosperity and success mark my journey to lasting wealth, Father. In Jesus' name.

10. Heavenly Father, I declare lasting wealth over my life. Let Your abundance overflow in every financial aspect, Lord. In Jesus' name.

11. Break the cycle of financial hardship, Lord. Establish me in lasting wealth that magnifies Your glory, Father. In Jesus' name.

12. Father, I trust You with my financial future. Let lasting wealth be a testament to Your unfailing love and provision. In Jesus' name.

13. Lord, open doors of lasting financial breakthroughs. Let Your favor shine upon my financial endeavors, Father. In Jesus' name.

14. Break every financial barrier, Lord. Establish me in lasting wealth that reflects Your abundance, Father. In Jesus' name.

15. Heavenly Father, I receive Your lasting financial blessings with gratitude. Let Your abundance overflow in every aspect of my life. In Jesus' name.

13.4. Prayer for Divine Multiplication

1. Heavenly Father, I bow before You, seeking Your divine multiplication in every area of my life. Multiply my efforts and endeavors, Lord, for Your glory. In Jesus' name.

2. Lord, let Your divine favor bring multiplication to my relationships, resources, and impact. Open doors of increase, Father. In Jesus' name.

3. Father, break every limitation hindering multiplication in my life. Propel me into a season of abundance and growth, Lord. In Jesus' name.

4. Lord, dismantle every obstacle blocking Your divine multiplication. Let Your grace multiply blessings beyond measure, Father. In Jesus' name.

5. Heavenly Father, I surrender my plans to You. Multiply my abilities and influence according to Your perfect plan, Lord. In Jesus' name.

6. Lord, I declare an end to mediocrity. Multiply my efforts to make a significant impact, Father. In Jesus' name.

7. Break every chain of stagnation, Lord. Multiply my influence to touch lives and spread Your love, Father. In Jesus' name.

8. Father, release divine wisdom and discernment as I navigate the path of multiplication. Guide my steps, Lord. In Jesus' name.

9. Lord, let Your divine multiplication distinguish me among my peers. Increase me in every area, Father. In Jesus' name.

10. Heavenly Father, I trust in Your timing for divine multiplication. Let patience and perseverance mark my journey, Lord. In Jesus' name.

11. Break the cycle of limitations, Lord. Multiply my impact and influence for Your kingdom, Father. In Jesus' name.

12. Father, I surrender my ambitions to You. Multiply my blessings to glorify Your name, Lord. In Jesus' name.

13. Lord, I declare an end to every setback. Multiply my successes and breakthroughs, Father. In Jesus' name.

14. Break every spirit of discouragement, Lord. Multiply my joy and optimism as I walk in Your divine plan, Father. In Jesus' name.

15. Heavenly Father, as I seek divine multiplication, let Your favor rest upon me. Multiply every aspect of my life for Your glory. In Jesus' name.

13.5. Prayer to Claim Divine Blessings

1. Heavenly Father, I come before You with gratitude, ready to claim Your divine blessings over my life. Shower me with Your favor, Lord, in Jesus' name.

2. Lord, break every barrier hindering Your blessings. Let Your abundance flow into my life, Father. In Jesus' name.

3. Father, I surrender my needs to You. Open the windows of heaven and pour out Your blessings, Lord. In Jesus' name.

4. Break the cycle of lack, Lord. Let Your divine blessings overflow in every area of my life, Father. In Jesus' name.

5. Heavenly Father, release Your blessings upon my family, relationships, and endeavors. Let Your provision surpass all our needs. In Jesus' name.

6. Lord, dismantle the stronghold of scarcity. Bless me abundantly, Father, that I may be a blessing to others. In Jesus' name.

7. Break every chain of limitation, Lord. Let Your divine blessings be a testimony to Your grace, Father. In Jesus' name.

8. Father, release me from the shackles of doubt and fear. Let Your blessings and favor be my inheritance, Lord. In Jesus' name.

9. Lord, bless the work of my hands. Let prosperity and success mark my journey in Your divine blessings, Father. In Jesus' name.

10. Heavenly Father, I declare Your divine blessings over my life. Let Your abundance overflow in every area, Lord. In Jesus' name.

11. Break the cycle of adversity, Lord. Let Your divine blessings overshadow every challenge, Father. In Jesus' name.

12. Father, I trust You with my present and future. Let Your blessings be a beacon of Your love and provision, Lord. In Jesus' name.

13. Lord, open doors of divine blessings. Let Your favor shine upon my endeavors, Father. In Jesus' name.

14. Break every financial barrier, Lord. Let Your blessings reign in every aspect of my life, Father. In Jesus' name.

15. Heavenly Father, I receive Your divine blessings with gratitude. Let Your goodness and mercy follow me all the days of my life. In Jesus' name.

13.6. Prayer for Godly Promotion

1. Heavenly Father, I humbly come before You, seeking Your divine favor for godly promotion. Lift me to new levels, Lord, in alignment with Your perfect plan. In Jesus' name.

2. Lord, let Your divine favor distinguish me. Open doors of opportunity and godly promotion, Father. In Jesus' name.

3. Father, break every chain hindering my godly promotion. Propel me to positions of influence and impact, Lord. In Jesus' name.

4. Lord, dismantle every obstacle blocking my path to godly promotion. Let Your grace lift me beyond my expectations, Father. In Jesus' name.

5. Heavenly Father, I surrender my ambitions to You. Promote me according to Your purpose, Lord. In Jesus' name.

6. Lord, I declare an end to mediocrity. Promote me to places of significance and positive influence, Father. In Jesus' name.

7. Break every chain of stagnation, Lord. Promote me to a level where Your glory shines brightly through my life. In Jesus' name.

8. Father, release divine wisdom and discernment as I navigate the path to godly promotion. Guide my steps, Lord. In Jesus' name.

9. Lord, let Your godly promotion distinguish me among my peers. Elevate me in every area of my life, Father. In Jesus' name.

10. Heavenly Father, I trust in Your timing for my godly promotion. Let patience and perseverance mark my journey, Lord. In Jesus' name.

11. Break the cycle of limitations, Lord. Promote me to places where I can make a positive impact for Your kingdom, Father. In Jesus' name.

12. Father, I surrender my ambitions to You. Promote me to places where I can glorify Your name and serve others, Lord. In Jesus' name.

13. Lord, I declare an end to setbacks. Promote me to realms of breakthroughs and accomplishments, Father. In Jesus' name.

14. Break every spirit of discouragement, Lord. Promote my spirit and fill me with hope for the godly promotion ahead, Father. In Jesus' name.

15. Heavenly Father, as I seek godly promotion, let Your favor rest upon me. Promote me in accordance with Your divine plan for my life. In Jesus' name.

13.7. Prayer for Easy Prosperity

1. Heavenly Father, I come before You with gratitude, seeking Your divine favor for easy prosperity. Let Your blessings flow effortlessly into my life, Lord, in Jesus' name.

2. Lord, break every cycle of financial struggle. Open doors of abundance and provide easy prosperity, Father. In Jesus' name.

3. Father, I surrender my financial endeavors to You. Establish me in easy prosperity that glorifies Your name. In Jesus' name.

4. Break every chain of financial instability, Lord. Let Your divine favor bring about easy prosperity in every area of my life, Father. In Jesus' name.

5. Heavenly Father, release Your financial favor upon me. Let easy prosperity be my portion, and may I be a conduit of blessings to others. In Jesus' name.

6. Lord, dismantle the stronghold of lack. Bless me abundantly, Father, that I may experience easy prosperity and be a blessing to those around me. In Jesus' name.

7. Break every chain of limitation, Lord. Let Your easy prosperity be a testimony to Your faithfulness and grace, Father. In Jesus' name.

8. Father, release me from the shackles of doubt and fear. Let easy prosperity and financial freedom be my inheritance. In Jesus' name.

9. Lord, bless the work of my hands. Let easy prosperity and success mark my journey, Father. In Jesus' name.

10. Heavenly Father, I declare easy prosperity over my life. Let Your abundance overflow effortlessly in every financial aspect, Lord. In Jesus' name.

11. Break the cycle of financial hardship, Lord. Establish me in easy prosperity that magnifies Your glory, Father. In Jesus' name.

12. Father, I trust You with my financial future. Let easy prosperity be a testament to Your unfailing love and provision, Lord. In Jesus' name.

13. Lord, open doors of easy financial breakthroughs. Let Your favor shine upon my financial endeavors, bringing forth prosperity with ease, Father. In Jesus' name.

14. Break every financial barrier, Lord. Let Your easy prosperity reign in every aspect of my life, Father. In Jesus' name.

15. Heavenly Father, I receive Your easy prosperity with gratitude. Let Your goodness and mercy follow me all the days of my life. In Jesus' name.

Chapter 14

Prayer Against Demonic Attacks

For our struggle is not against flesh and blood, but against the rulers, against the authorities, against the powers of this dark world and against the spiritual forces of evil in the heavenly realms.

Ephesians 6:12 (NIV)

14.1. Prayer to Terminate Demonic Curses

1. Heavenly Father, I approach Your throne seeking deliverance from demonic curses. Let Your mighty hand terminate every curse affecting my life, Lord. In Jesus' name.

2. Lord, break the chains of demonic influence. Let Your power nullify every curse and release me into freedom, Father. In Jesus' name.

3. Father, I renounce every demonic attachment. Let the blood of Jesus erase every curse and grant me divine protection, Lord. In Jesus' name.

4. Break every generational curse, Lord. Let Your cleansing power remove every mark of the enemy from my life, Father. In Jesus' name.

5. Heavenly Father, I declare my allegiance to You. Let Your authority break the grip of demonic curses and release me into divine favor, Lord. In Jesus' name.

6. Lord, dismantle every altar of darkness. Let Your consuming fire destroy every curse spoken against me, Father. In Jesus' name.

7. Break the cycle of curses, Lord. Let Your healing touch remove every affliction caused by demonic influences, Father. In Jesus' name.

8. Father, release me from the snares of the enemy. Let Your light dispel every darkness and terminate every demonic curse, Lord. In Jesus' name.

9. Lord, I surrender to Your authority. Let Your word be a shield against every demonic curse, granting me freedom and restoration, Father. In Jesus' name.

10. Heavenly Father, I rebuke every curse in the name of Jesus. Let Your blood cleanse me from every evil attachment, Lord. In Jesus' name.

11. Break every soul tie with the enemy, Lord. Let Your power terminate every demonic curse and release me into Your divine blessings, Father. In Jesus' name.

12. Father, I plead the blood of Jesus over my life. Let Your protective shield terminate every demonic curse, granting me peace and victory, Lord. In Jesus' name.

13. Lord, I renounce every pact with darkness. Let Your redeeming power terminate every demonic curse and establish me in Your freedom, Father. In Jesus' name.

14. Break the influence of demonic spirits, Lord. Let Your deliverance terminate every curse and release me into a life of abundance, Father. In Jesus' name.

15. Heavenly Father, I receive Your deliverance with gratitude. Let Your grace terminate every demonic curse and establish me in Your divine protection, Lord. In Jesus' name.

14.2. Prayer Against Witchcraft Attacks

1. Heavenly Father, I stand firm against the forces of witchcraft. Let Your divine shield protect me from every attack, Lord. In Jesus' name.

2. Lord, break every enchantment and spell cast against me. Let Your powerful hand nullify the effects of witchcraft attacks, Father. In Jesus' name.

3. Father, I surrender my life to Your protection. Let Your angels guard me against every form of witchcraft assault, Lord. In Jesus' name.

4. Break the influence of every witchcraft spirit, Lord. Let Your blood cleanse me and render every evil plan powerless, Father. In Jesus' name.

5. Heavenly Father, I declare Your authority over my life. Let every weapon formed by witchcraft be disarmed by Your mighty hand, Lord. In Jesus' name.

6. Lord, dismantle every altar of witchcraft. Let Your consuming fire destroy every evil work plotted against me, Father. In Jesus' name.

7. Break the cycle of witchcraft attacks, Lord. Let Your protective shield deflect every arrow and scheme of the enemy, Father. In Jesus' name.

8. Father, release me from the snares of witchcraft. Let Your light dispel every darkness and render every curse ineffective, Lord. In Jesus' name.

9. Lord, I plead the blood of Jesus over my life. Let Your redeeming power shield me from every witchcraft attack and establish me in Your peace, Father. In Jesus' name.

10. Heavenly Father, I rebuke every witchcraft spirit. Let Your word be a fortress, breaking every curse and releasing me into freedom, Lord. In Jesus' name.

11. Break every soul tie with witchcraft, Lord. Let Your power terminate every attack and release me into victory and breakthrough, Father. In Jesus' name.

12. Father, I renounce every pact with darkness. Let Your redeeming power render every weapon of witchcraft useless, Lord. In Jesus' name.

13. Lord, I declare my allegiance to You. Let Your angels encamp around me, guarding against every witchcraft assault, Father. In Jesus' name.

14. Break the influence of every witchcraft covenant, Lord. Let Your deliverance terminate every attack and establish me in Your divine protection, Father. In Jesus' name.

15. Heavenly Father, I receive Your deliverance with gratitude. Let Your grace shield me from every witchcraft attack and establish me in Your victory, Lord. In Jesus' name.

14.3. Prayer Against Household Attacks

1. Heavenly Father, I lift my household before You, seeking protection against every form of attack. Let Your divine shield guard us, Lord. In Jesus' name.

2. Lord, break every cycle of negativity and harm in my household. Let Your powerful hand nullify every plot and scheme of the enemy, Father. In Jesus' name.

3. Father, I surrender my family to Your protection. Let Your angels encamp around us, guarding against every form of attack, Lord. In Jesus' name.

4. Break the influence of every negative spirit, Lord. Let Your blood cleanse my household and render every evil plan powerless, Father. In Jesus' name.

5. Heavenly Father, I declare Your authority over my family. Let every weapon formed against us be disarmed by Your mighty hand, Lord. In Jesus' name.

6. Lord, dismantle every altar of darkness in my household. Let Your consuming fire destroy every evil work plotted against us, Father. In Jesus' name.

7. Break the cycle of attacks, Lord. Let Your protective shield deflect every arrow and scheme of the enemy in my household, Father. In Jesus' name.

8. Father, release my family from the snares of negativity. Let Your light dispel every darkness and render every curse ineffective, Lord. In Jesus' name.

9. Lord, I plead the blood of Jesus over my family. Let Your redeeming power shield us from every form of attack and establish us in Your peace, Father. In Jesus' name.

10. Heavenly Father, I rebuke every negative spirit. Let Your word be a fortress, breaking every curse and releasing my family into freedom, Lord. In Jesus' name.

11. Break every soul tie with negativity, Lord. Let Your power terminate every attack and release my family into victory and breakthrough, Father. In Jesus' name.

12. Father, we renounce every pact with darkness. Let Your redeeming power render every weapon of attack useless, Lord. In Jesus' name.

13. Lord, we declare our allegiance to You. Let Your angels encamp around us, guarding against every form of attack, Father. In Jesus' name.

14. Break the influence of every negative covenant, Lord. Let Your deliverance terminate every attack and establish my family in Your divine protection, Father. In Jesus' name.

15. Heavenly Father, we receive Your deliverance with gratitude. Let Your grace shield my family from every form of attack and establish us in Your victory, Lord. In Jesus' name.

Chapter 15

Prayer To Invoke The Crying Blood Of Jesus

In him, we have redemption through his blood, the forgiveness of sins, in accordance with the riches of God's grace."

Ephesians 1:7

15.1. Prayer to Silence Evil Blood

1. Lord, silence every evil blood crying against me. Let Your mercy speak louder. In Jesus' name.

2. Break every curse linked to ancestral blood. Let Your redeeming power prevail. In Jesus' name.

3. Father, cleanse my bloodline from every evil contamination. Let Your purity reign. In Jesus' name.

4. Break the power of negative blood connections. Let Your blood speak better things. In Jesus' name.

5. Lord, sever ties with every evil blood covenant. Let Your covenant of grace prevail. In Jesus' name.

6. Release me from the grip of ancestral bloodline curses. Let Your freedom reign. In Jesus' name.

7. Father, let the blood of Jesus silence every accusation. Let Your covering be my shield. In Jesus' name.

8. Break the cycle of generational bloodline afflictions. Let Your healing flow. In Jesus' name.

9. Lord, release Your cleansing power on my bloodline. Let Your mercy speak for us. In Jesus' name.

10. Break every curse attached to my blood. Let the blood of Jesus speak victory. In Jesus' name.

11. Father, purify my blood from every contamination. Let Your sanctification be my shield. In Jesus' name.

12. Release me from every negative blood connection. Let Your redemption prevail. In Jesus' name.

13. Lord, cleanse my blood from every ancestral curse. Let Your restoration flow. In Jesus' name.

14. Break the influence of every evil blood covenant. Let Your deliverance reign. In Jesus' name.

15. Father, let the blood of Jesus silence every voice of accusation. Let Your vindication be my testimony. In Jesus' name.

15.2. Prayer to Invoke the Crying Blood of Jesus

1. Heavenly Father, I invoke the crying blood of Jesus over my life. Let it speak mercy and redemption. In Jesus' name.

2. Lord, let the crying blood of Jesus silence every accusation against me. Let it declare my innocence. In Jesus' name.

3. Father, I plead the crying blood of Jesus to break every curse. Let it speak deliverance and freedom. In Jesus' name.

4. Break the power of negativity with the crying blood of Jesus. Let it declare my victory. In Jesus' name.

5. Lord, let the crying blood of Jesus sever every negative blood connection. Let it bring cleansing and purity. In Jesus' name.

6. Release me from ancestral afflictions through the crying blood of Jesus. Let it speak healing. In Jesus' name.

7. Father, let the crying blood of Jesus break every generational curse. Let it speak restoration. In Jesus' name.

8. Lord, cleanse and purify my bloodline with the crying blood of Jesus. Let it declare sanctification. In Jesus' name.

9. Break every negative covenant with the crying blood of Jesus. Let it speak deliverance. In Jesus' name.

10. Lord, let the crying blood of Jesus release me from ancestral bondages. Let it speak freedom. In Jesus' name.

11. Father, I invoke the crying blood of Jesus to cleanse my blood from every contamination. Let it declare redemption. In Jesus' name.

12. Break the grip of every evil blood covenant with the crying blood of Jesus. Let it speak victory. In Jesus' name.

13. Lord, let the crying blood of Jesus silence every voice of accusation. Let it declare my innocence. In Jesus' name.

14. Father, I plead the crying blood of Jesus over my family. Let it break every curse and speak deliverance. In Jesus' name.

15. Heavenly Father, we invoke the crying blood of Jesus. Let it speak mercy, redemption, and victory over our lives. In Jesus' name.

15.3. Prayer to Battle with the Blood of Jesus

1. Heavenly Father, I enter the battle covered by the powerful blood of Jesus. Let it shield me. In Jesus' name.

2. Lord, let the blood of Jesus be my defense in the spiritual warfare. Cover me, Father. In Jesus' name.

3. Father, I plead the blood of Jesus as my weapon against every evil force. Let it prevail. In Jesus' name.

4. Break the influence of darkness with the battling blood of Jesus. Let it secure victory. In Jesus' name.

5. Lord, let the blood of Jesus be my refuge in the battle. Cover me with Your protection. In Jesus' name.

6. Release Your power through the blood of Jesus to conquer every spiritual enemy. Let it prevail. In Jesus' name.

7. Father, I declare the authority of the blood of Jesus in this battle. Let it overcome. In Jesus' name.

8. Lord, let the blood of Jesus dismantle every evil plot. Be my shield, Father. In Jesus' name.

9. Break every chain with the battling blood of Jesus. Let it bring freedom and victory. In Jesus' name.

10. Lord, I invoke the blood of Jesus to defeat every spiritual opposition. Let it secure my triumph. In Jesus' name.

11. Father, let the blood of Jesus speak against every weapon formed. Let it prevail. In Jesus' name.

12. Lord, cover me with the battling blood of Jesus. Let it be my armor in this spiritual warfare. In Jesus' name.

13. Release the power of the blood of Jesus to crush every stronghold. Let it bring deliverance. In Jesus' name.

14. Father, I plead the blood of Jesus over my mind, heart, and spirit. Let it be my fortress. In Jesus' name.

15. Heavenly Father, let the battling blood of Jesus be my victory in every spiritual conflict. In Jesus' name.

Chapter 16

Prayer Against Determined Enemies

Deliver me from my enemies, O God; be my fortress against those who are attacking me. Deliver me from evildoers and save me from those who are after my blood.

Psalm 59:1-2 (NIV)

16.1. Prayer Against Unyielding Enemies

1. Heavenly Father, I stand against unyielding enemies, invoking Your power. Let Your might scatter their plans. In Jesus' name.

2. Lord, thwart the schemes of unyielding adversaries. Let Your hand intervene on my behalf. In Jesus' name.

3. Father, break the persistence of my enemies. Let Your consuming fire disrupt their strategies. In Jesus' name.

4. Lord, I declare Your authority against unyielding foes. Let Your word confound their efforts. In Jesus' name.

5. Break the stubbornness of my adversaries, Lord. Let Your justice prevail over their persistence. In Jesus' name.

6. Father, dismantle the resilience of my enemies. Let Your divine intervention scatter their plans. In Jesus' name.

7. Lord, silence the unyielding opposition. Let Your peace reign in the midst of turmoil. In Jesus' name.

8. Break the tenacity of my enemies, Father. Let Your victorious hand crush their resistance. In Jesus' name.

9. Lord, I stand against unyielding adversaries. Let Your divine light expose and scatter their darkness. In Jesus' name.

10. Father, confound the strategies of unyielding foes. Let Your wisdom prevail over their schemes. In Jesus' name.

11. Lord, release Your consuming fire against unyielding opposition. Let Your power overcome their resistance. In Jesus' name.

12. Break the stubborn persistence of my enemies, Father. Let Your favor surround and protect me. In Jesus' name.

13. Lord, I plead for Your intervention against unyielding foes. Let Your mighty hand scatter their plans. In Jesus' name.

14. Father, silence the voices of unyielding adversaries. Let Your peace reign in my life. In Jesus' name.

15. Heavenly Father, I declare Your sovereignty over unyielding enemies. Let Your triumph be evident in my life. In Jesus' name.

16.2. Prayer Against Unrepentant Enemies

1. Heavenly Father, I stand against unrepentant enemies seeking to harm me. Let Your mercy soften their hearts. In Jesus' name.

2. Lord, touch the hearts of unrepentant adversaries. Let Your love break through their hardness. In Jesus' name.

3. Father, I pray for the repentance of my enemies. Let Your grace lead them to transformation. In Jesus' name.

4. Lord, break the unrepentant spirit of my adversaries. Let Your conviction lead them to Your mercy. In Jesus' name.

5. Father, I lift up my enemies before You. Soften their hearts, Lord, and lead them to repentance. In Jesus' name.

6. Lord, I declare Your love over unrepentant foes. Let Your grace draw them to repentance. In Jesus' name.

7. Break the unrepentant spirit in my enemies, Father. Let Your forgiveness be their path to change. In Jesus' name.

8. Lord, I pray for the repentance of those who seek my harm. Let Your mercy lead them to transformation. In Jesus' name.

9. Father, touch the hearts of unrepentant adversaries. Let Your love break through and lead them to change. In Jesus' name.

10. Lord, break the hardness in the hearts of my enemies. Let Your Holy Spirit guide them to repentance. In Jesus' name.

11. Father, I intercede for the repentance of my adversaries. Let Your grace lead them to a life of transformation. In Jesus' name.

12. Lord, soften the hearts of unrepentant foes. Let Your mercy draw them to You. In Jesus' name.

13. Break the unrepentant spirit in my enemies, Father. Let Your conviction lead them to Your forgiveness. In Jesus' name.

14. Lord, I plead for the repentance of those against me. Let Your love overwhelm their hearts. In Jesus' name.

15. Heavenly Father, I stand against unrepentant enemies. Let Your mercy and grace lead them to change. In Jesus' name.

16.3. Prayer to Overcome Your Enemies

1. Heavenly Father, I come before You to seek Your strength and guidance to overcome my enemies. In Jesus' name.

2. Lord, empower me to rise above the challenges posed by my adversaries. Let Your victory be my shield. In Jesus' name.

3. Father, I declare that no weapon formed against me shall prosper. Let Your favor surround and protect me. In Jesus' name.

4. Lord, break the schemes of my enemies. Let Your wisdom guide me to victory. In Jesus' name.

5. Father, I trust in Your strength to overcome every obstacle. Let Your grace be my source of resilience. In Jesus' name.

6. Lord, I release my burdens to You. Grant me the courage and wisdom to conquer my enemies. In Jesus' name.

7. Father, silence the voices of opposition around me. Let Your peace reign in the midst of turmoil. In Jesus' name.

8. Lord, I cast my anxieties on You. Grant me the strength to face and overcome my adversaries. In Jesus' name.

9. Father, lead me in paths of righteousness. Let Your light expose and dispel the darkness of my enemies. In Jesus' name.

10. Lord, I declare Your victory over every challenge. Let Your name be glorified in my triumph. In Jesus' name.

11. Father, grant me discernment to navigate through the schemes of my enemies. Let Your wisdom guide my steps. In Jesus' name.

12. Lord, break the chains of negativity surrounding me. Let Your freedom reign in my life. In Jesus' name.

13. Father, empower me with resilience to face and conquer my enemies. Let Your strength be my anchor. In Jesus' name.

14. Lord, I trust in Your promises of protection. Let Your angels encamp around me against my adversaries. In Jesus' name.

15. Heavenly Father, I declare victory over my enemies through Your strength. Let Your name be glorified in my triumph. In Jesus' name.

16.4. Prayer Against the Enemies of Christ in You

1.   Heavenly Father, I stand in Your presence, covered by the blood of Jesus. I rebuke and resist every enemy of Christ within me. In Jesus' name.

2.   Lord, I declare that I am a temple of the Holy Spirit. Every enemy of Christ within me must bow to Your authority. In Jesus' name.

3.   Father, I plead the precious blood of Jesus against every influence that opposes Christ in me. Let Your power prevail. In Jesus' name.

4.   Lord, I declare that I am crucified with Christ. Every enemy of His presence within me is nullified. In Jesus' name.

5.   Father, I renounce and reject every foothold the enemy seeks within my spirit. I am a vessel of Christ. In Jesus' name.

6.   Lord, I invite the Holy Spirit to fill every corner of my being, pushing out any influence contrary to Christ. In Jesus' name.

7.   Father, I take authority over every thought, desire, and motive that opposes Christ within me. Let Your light shine. In Jesus' name.

8. Lord, cleanse and sanctify me from within. Let every enemy of Christ be expelled from my heart. In Jesus' name.

9. Father, I surrender my will to Yours. Let the enemies of Christ within me submit to the lordship of Jesus. In Jesus' name.

10. Lord, I stand firm in the truth of Your Word. Every enemy of Christ within me is defeated by the power of His resurrection. In Jesus' name.

11. Father, I close every door that the enemy could use to infiltrate my soul. I am sealed by the blood of Jesus. In Jesus' name.

12. Lord, I put on the full armor of God to resist the enemies of Christ within me. Let Your strength be my defense. In Jesus' name.

13. Father, let the fire of the Holy Spirit burn away any impurity within me. Every enemy of Christ must flee. In Jesus' name.

14. Lord, I surrender my weaknesses to You. Strengthen me against the enemies of Christ seeking to undermine my faith. In Jesus' name.

15. Heavenly Father, I declare that Christ reigns supreme within me. Every enemy is subdued by His authority. In Jesus' name.

16.5. Prayer Against Destructive Enemies

1. Heavenly Father, I come before You in the name of Jesus, seeking Your protection from destructive enemies. Shield me with Your divine armor. In Jesus' name.

2. Lord, I declare Your authority over every destructive plot formed against me. Let Your angels surround and defend me. In Jesus' name.

3. Father, I plead the blood of Jesus as my shield against destructive enemies. Let Your favor guard me from harm. In Jesus' name.

4. Lord, break the influence of destructive forces seeking to harm me. Let Your light expose and dispel their darkness. In Jesus' name.

5. Father, I stand firm in Your promises of protection. Every weapon formed against me shall not prosper. In Jesus' name.

6. Lord, dismantle the plans of destructive adversaries. Let Your wisdom guide me to safety. In Jesus' name.

7. Father, I release the power of Your Word against every destructive assignment. Let Your truth be my defense. In Jesus' name.

8. Lord, I declare Your peace over my life. Silence the voices of destruction around me. In Jesus' name.

9. Father, I rebuke every spirit of destruction assigned against me. Let Your grace lead me to safety. In Jesus' name.

10. Lord, break the chains of negativity and destruction. Let Your freedom reign in my life. In Jesus' name.

11. Father, I trust in Your strength to overcome destructive enemies. Let Your victory be evident in my life. In Jesus' name.

12. Lord, I declare Your protection over my family, home, and endeavors. Let Your angels encamp around us. In Jesus' name.

13. Father, I stand against every destructive plan. Let Your divine intervention scatter the schemes of my enemies. In Jesus' name.

14. Lord, I plead for Your mercy and protection. Guard me against destructive forces seeking my downfall. In Jesus' name.

15. Heavenly Father, I declare Your sovereignty over destructive enemies. Let Your peace reign in the midst of turmoil. In Jesus' name.

16.6. Prayer to Overpower Stubborn Enemies

1. Heavenly Father, I come before Your throne of grace, seeking Your divine intervention to overpower my stubborn enemies. In Jesus' name.

2. Lord, I declare Your authority over every stubborn adversary in my life. Let Your power subdue them completely. In Jesus' name.

3. Father, I plead the blood of Jesus against every stubborn opposition. Let Your victory prevail over their resistance. In Jesus' name.

4. Lord, break the stubbornness of my enemies. Let Your Holy Spirit soften their hearts to Your truth. In Jesus' name.

5. Father, I stand on the promises of Your Word. Overpower every stubborn enemy with Your unchanging truth. In Jesus' name.

6. Lord, I release the fire of the Holy Spirit to consume the stubborn resistance of my adversaries. Let Your presence overwhelm them. In Jesus' name.

7. Father, I trust in Your strength to overcome the stubborn challenges before me. Let Your triumph be evident in my life. In Jesus' name.

8. Lord, dismantle the stubborn schemes and plans of my enemies. Let Your wisdom guide me to victory. In Jesus' name.

9. Father, I rebuke every spirit of stubborn opposition. Let Your grace lead them to surrender to Your will. In Jesus' name.

10. Lord, break the chains of stubborn negativity and resistance. Let Your freedom reign in my life. In Jesus' name.

11. Father, I declare Your power over the stubborn obstacles hindering my progress. Let Your favor open doors of breakthrough. In Jesus' name.

12. Lord, I trust in Your promises of protection. Overpower every stubborn force seeking to undermine my journey. In Jesus' name.

13. Father, I stand against every stubborn plan. Let Your divine intervention scatter the schemes of my enemies. In Jesus' name.

14. Lord, I plead for Your mercy and intervention. Overpower every stubborn force with Your divine grace. In Jesus' name.

15. Heavenly Father, I declare Your sovereignty over stubborn enemies. Let Your peace reign in the midst of the battle. In Jesus' name.

16.7. Prayer to Thwart Enemies' Plans

1. Heavenly Father, I come before You with a heart full of trust, seeking Your divine intervention to thwart the plans of my enemies. In Jesus' name.

2. Lord, I declare Your authority over every scheme and plot formed against me. Let Your wisdom and discernment expose and thwart their every plan. In Jesus' name.

3. Father, I plead the blood of Jesus as a protective shield against the machinations of my enemies. Let Your favor confound and thwart their evil intentions. In Jesus' name.

4. Lord, break the influence of every deceptive spirit working in the hearts of those planning harm. Thwart their plans with Your truth. In Jesus' name.

5. Father, I stand firm in the promises of Your Word. Thwart every plan formed against me with the power of Your unchanging truth. In Jesus' name.

6. Lord, I release the fire of the Holy Spirit to consume and thwart the hidden agendas of my adversaries. Let Your presence overwhelm and dismantle their plans. In Jesus' name.

7. Father, I trust in Your strength to overturn and thwart the cunning schemes devised by my enemies. Let Your victory be evident in my life. In Jesus' name.

8. Lord, dismantle the secret plans and strategies of my enemies. Let Your wisdom guide me to discern and thwart their every move. In Jesus' name.

9. Father, I rebuke every spirit of deception and manipulation operating in the plans of my enemies. Thwart their schemes with Your divine intervention. In Jesus' name.

10. Lord, break the chains of darkness that surround the plotting of my adversaries. Thwart their plans, and let Your freedom reign in my life. In Jesus' name.

11. Father, I declare Your power over every plot designed to hinder my progress. Thwart the schemes of my enemies, and let Your favor open doors of breakthrough. In Jesus' name.

12. Lord, I trust in Your promises of protection. Thwart the hidden strategies of my enemies seeking to undermine my journey. In Jesus' name.

13. Father, I stand against every deceptive plan. Thwart the schemes of my enemies, and let Your divine intervention scatter their plots. In Jesus' name.

14. Lord, I plead for Your mercy and intervention. Thwart every hidden agenda with Your divine grace. In Jesus' name.

15. Heavenly Father, I declare Your sovereignty over the plans of my enemies. Thwart their schemes, and let Your peace reign in the midst of the battle. In Jesus' name.

16.8. Prayer to Expose Enemies' Secrets

1. Heavenly Father, I come before Your throne of grace, seeking Your divine intervention to expose the secrets of my enemies. In Jesus' name.

2. Lord, I declare Your authority over every hidden agenda and secret plot formed against me. Let Your light shine and expose the darkness. In Jesus' name.

3. Father, I plead the blood of Jesus as a discerning shield against the secrecy of my enemies. Let Your favor reveal and uncover their hidden schemes. In Jesus' name.

4. Lord, break the veil of secrecy surrounding the deceptive plans. Let Your Holy Spirit bring to light every hidden intention. In Jesus' name.

5. Father, I stand firm in the promises of Your Word. Expose every secret plot formed against me with the power of Your unchanging truth. In Jesus' name.

6. Lord, I release the fire of the Holy Spirit to consume and reveal the hidden agendas of my adversaries. Let Your presence overwhelm and expose their secrets. In Jesus' name.

7. Father, I trust in Your strength to uncover and expose the cunning secrets devised by my enemies. Let Your revelation be evident in my life. In Jesus' name.

8. Lord, dismantle the covert plans and strategies of my enemies. Let Your wisdom guide me to discern and expose their every move. In Jesus' name.

9. Father, I rebuke every spirit of deception and secrecy operating in the plans of my enemies. Expose their hidden schemes with Your divine intervention. In Jesus' name.

10. Lord, break the chains of darkness that surround the secretive plotting of my adversaries. Expose their secrets, and let Your truth reign in my life. In Jesus' name.

11. Father, I declare Your power over every concealed plan designed to hinder my progress. Expose the secrets of my enemies, and let Your favor open doors of breakthrough. In Jesus' name.

12. Lord, I trust in Your promises of protection. Expose the hidden strategies of my enemies seeking to undermine my journey. In Jesus' name.

13. Father, I stand against every deceptive secret. Expose the hidden agendas of my enemies, and let Your divine intervention scatter their concealed plots. In Jesus' name.

14. Lord, I plead for Your mercy and revelation. Expose every concealed agenda with Your divine grace. In Jesus' name.

15. Heavenly Father, I declare Your sovereignty over the secrets of my enemies. Expose their hidden schemes, and let Your peace reign in the midst of the revelation. In Jesus' name.

Chapter 17

Prayer Against Water Spirit

"When you pass through the waters, I will be with you; and when you pass through the rivers, they will not sweep over you. When you walk through the fire, you will not be burned; the flames will not set you ablaze."

Isaiah 43:2 (NIV)

17.1. Prayer Against Water Spirits

1. Lord, I rebuke water spirits attacking my life. Let Your fire consume their influence. In Jesus' name.

2. Father, break the power of water spirits. Let Your light dispel their darkness. In Jesus' name.

3. Lord, I declare freedom from water spirits. Let Your waves of deliverance flow. In Jesus' name.

4. Father, drown every water spirit plotting harm. Let Your victory prevail. In Jesus' name.

5. Lord, I reject water spirits' influence. Let Your living water cleanse and protect. In Jesus' name.

6. Father, dismantle water spirits' strongholds. Let Your current of grace prevail. In Jesus' name.

7. Lord, I declare authority over water spirits. Let Your river of life flow. In Jesus' name.

8. Father, wash away the schemes of water spirits. Let Your cleansing flood prevail. In Jesus' name.

9. Lord, I rebuke every flood of attack. Let Your peace overcome. In Jesus' name.

10. Father, break the chains of water spirits. Let Your living water bring freedom. In Jesus' name.

11. Lord, I declare victory over water spirits. Let Your waves of protection surround. In Jesus' name.

12. Father, quench the fiery darts of water spirits. Let Your living water shield. In Jesus' name.

13. Lord, I plead the blood against water spirits. Let Your river of life prevail. In Jesus' name.

14. Father, silence the voices of water spirits. Let Your still waters restore. In Jesus' name.

15. Lord, I release the authority of Your name against water spirits. Let Your living water reign. In Jesus' name.

17.2. Prayer Against Arrows of Water Spirits

1. Heavenly Father, I stand before Your throne, seeking protection against the arrows of water spirits. In Jesus' name.

2. Lord, I declare Your authority over the arrows launched by water spirits. Let Your shield intercept every attack. In Jesus' name.

3. Father, I plead the blood of Jesus as a powerful defense against the arrows of water spirits. Let Your divine protection surround me. In Jesus' name.

4. Lord, break the influence of every arrow sent by water spirits. Let Your angels disarm and destroy their weaponry. In Jesus' name.

5. Father, I stand firm in the promises of Your Word. Nullify the impact of every arrow with the power of Your unchanging truth. In Jesus' name.

6. Lord, I release the fire of the Holy Spirit to consume and dissolve the arrows of water spirits. Let Your presence overwhelm and dismantle their attacks. In Jesus' name.

7. Father, I trust in Your strength to deflect and thwart the arrows aimed at me. Let Your victory be evident in my life. In Jesus' name.

8. Lord, dismantle the plans behind the arrows of water spirits. Let Your wisdom guide me to discern and counter their every move. In Jesus' name.

9. Father, I rebuke every spirit behind the arrows. Let Your divine intervention scatter their plans and render their arrows powerless. In Jesus' name.

10. Lord, break the chains of darkness associated with the arrows of water spirits. Let Your light dispel their plots and bring forth freedom. In Jesus' name.

11. Father, I declare Your power over every arrow designed to hinder my progress. Neutralize the impact of water spirits' arrows, and let Your favor open doors of breakthrough. In Jesus' name.

12. Lord, I trust in Your promises of protection. Guard me against the arrows of water spirits seeking to undermine my journey. In Jesus' name.

13. Father, I stand against every destructive arrow. Let Your divine intervention expose and nullify the arrows of water spirits. In Jesus' name.

14. Lord, I plead for Your mercy and intervention. Render every arrow of water spirits harmless with Your divine grace. In Jesus' name.

15. Heavenly Father, I declare Your sovereignty over the arrows of water spirits. Disarm and neutralize their attacks, and let Your peace reign in the midst of the battle. In Jesus' name.

17.3. Prayer to Break Evil Soul-Ties

1. Heavenly Father, I come before You, seeking liberation from every evil soul-tie. In Jesus' name.

2. Lord, I declare Your authority over every ungodly connection binding my soul. Break and release me. In Jesus' name.

3. Father, I plead the blood of Jesus to sever and cleanse me from every evil soul-tie. Let Your healing flow. In Jesus' name.

4. Lord, break the influence of every ungodly soul-tie in my life. Let Your freedom reign. In Jesus' name.

5. Father, I stand firm in the promises of Your Word. Break every ungodly connection with the power of Your truth. In Jesus' name.

6. Lord, I release the fire of the Holy Spirit to burn away every evil soul-tie. Let Your purifying presence prevail. In Jesus' name.

7. Father, I trust in Your strength to break and release me from every ungodly soul-tie. Let Your victory be evident in my life. In Jesus' name.

8. Lord, dismantle the chains of every unhealthy soul-tie. Let Your wisdom guide me to discern and break free. In Jesus' name.

9. Father, I rebuke every spirit associated with ungodly soul-ties. Let Your divine intervention sever and release me. In Jesus' name.

10. Lord, break the bondage of every ungodly soul-tie. Let Your liberating power bring forth freedom. In Jesus' name.

11. Father, I declare Your power over every soul-tie designed to hinder my progress. Break and release me, and let Your favor open doors of breakthrough. In Jesus' name.

12. Lord, I trust in Your promises of deliverance. Break and release me from every ungodly soul-tie seeking to undermine my journey. In Jesus' name.

13. Father, I stand against every entanglement. Let Your divine intervention break and release me from every evil soul-tie. In Jesus' name.

14. Lord, I plead for Your mercy and release. Break every ungodly soul-tie with Your divine grace. In Jesus' name.

15. Heavenly Father, I declare Your sovereignty over my soul. Break and release me from every evil soul-tie, and let Your peace reign in my heart. In Jesus' name.

18. Breaking Free From Spiritual Marriage

Chapter 18

Prayer Against Spirit Marriage

For our struggle is not against flesh and blood, but against the rulers, against the authorities, against the powers of this dark world and against the spiritual forces of evil in the heavenly realms.

Psalm 91:4-5 (NIV)

18.1. Breaking Free From Spiritual Marriage

1. Heavenly Father, I come before You, seeking liberation from any spiritual marriage. In Jesus' name.

2. Lord, I declare Your authority over any unholy spiritual union. Break and release me. In Jesus' name.

3. Father, I plead the blood of Jesus to sever and cleanse me from any spiritual marriage. Let Your healing flow. In Jesus' name.

4. Lord, break the influence of any spiritual marriage in my life. Let Your freedom reign. In Jesus' name.

5. Father, I stand firm in the promises of Your Word. Break every ungodly connection with the power of Your truth. In Jesus' name.

6. Lord, I release the fire of the Holy Spirit to burn away any spiritual entanglement. Let Your purifying presence prevail. In Jesus' name.

7. Father, I trust in Your strength to break and release me from any spiritual marriage. Let Your victory be evident in my life. In Jesus' name.

8. Lord, dismantle the chains of any unholy spiritual union. Let Your wisdom guide me to discern and break free. In Jesus' name.

9. Father, I rebuke every spirit associated with any spiritual marriage. Let Your divine intervention sever and release me. In Jesus' name.

10. Lord, break the bondage of any spiritual marriage. Let Your liberating power bring forth freedom. In Jesus' name.

11. Father, I declare Your power over any spiritual entanglement designed to hinder my progress. Break and release me, and let Your favor open doors of breakthrough. In Jesus' name.

12. Lord, I trust in Your promises of deliverance. Break and release me from any spiritual marriage seeking to undermine my journey. In Jesus' name.

13. Father, I stand against any spiritual entanglement. Let Your divine intervention break and release me. In Jesus' name.

14. Lord, I plead for Your mercy and release. Break any spiritual marriage with Your divine grace. In Jesus' name.

15. Heavenly Father, I declare Your sovereignty over my life. Break and release me from any spiritual marriage, and let Your peace reign in my heart. In Jesus' name.

18.2. Prayer to Restore and Heal Your Marriage

1. Heavenly Father, I come before You, seeking Your divine intervention to restore and heal my marriage. In Jesus' name.

2. Lord, I acknowledge Your sovereignty over relationships. Heal the wounds and restore the love in my marriage. In Jesus' name.

3. Father, I plead the blood of Jesus over my marriage. Let Your healing power flow and mend every broken aspect. In Jesus' name.

4. Lord, break down the walls of misunderstanding and strife in my marriage. Let Your peace reign and bring restoration. In Jesus' name.

5. Father, I stand on Your promises for marriages. Revive the love, trust, and unity in my relationship. In Jesus' name.

6. Lord, I release forgiveness into my marriage. Let Your grace mend the brokenness and restore harmony. In Jesus' name.

7. Father, I invite Your Spirit to work in the hearts of my spouse and me. Bring healing and unity to our marriage. In Jesus' name.

8. Lord, dismantle the strongholds of discord and resentment. Let Your wisdom guide us to reconciliation. In Jesus' name.

9. Father, I rebuke every spirit of division. Let Your divine intervention bring healing and restoration to my marriage. In Jesus' name.

10. Lord, break the chains of bitterness and unforgiveness. Let Your liberating power bring forth a new beginning in my marriage. In Jesus' name.

11. Father, I declare Your power over the challenges in my marriage. Break and release us from any hindrance to restoration. In Jesus' name.

12. Lord, I trust in Your promises of reconciliation. Restore the joy and commitment in our marriage. In Jesus' name.

13. Father, I stand against any external influence affecting my marriage negatively. Let Your divine intervention protect and restore. In Jesus' name.

14. Lord, I plead for Your mercy and healing touch. Restore my marriage with Your divine grace. In Jesus' name.

15. Heavenly Father, I surrender my marriage to You. Let Your restoration and healing flow, and may our union reflect Your love and glory. In Jesus' name.

18.3. Prayer for Peace in Marriage

1. Heavenly Father, I humbly come before You, seeking Your divine peace to reign in my marriage. In Jesus' name.

2. Lord, I acknowledge You as the source of true peace. Let Your calming presence fill our home and hearts. In Jesus' name.

3. Father, I plead the blood of Jesus over my marriage. Let Your peace guard our minds and hearts. In Jesus' name.

4. Lord, break down the walls of tension and discord in my marriage. Let Your peace reign and bring serenity. In Jesus' name.

5. Father, I stand on Your promises for peace. Dispel anxiety and bring tranquility to our relationship. In Jesus' name.

6. Lord, I release forgiveness and understanding into my marriage. Let Your grace foster an atmosphere of peace. In Jesus' name.

7. Father, I invite Your Spirit to work in the hearts of my spouse and me. Bring peace and unity to our home. In Jesus' name.

8. Lord, dismantle the strongholds of arguments and strife. Let Your wisdom guide us to a harmonious relationship. In Jesus' name.

9. Father, I rebuke every spirit of discord. Let Your divine intervention bring peace and understanding to my marriage. In Jesus' name.

10. Lord, break the chains of misunderstandings and conflicts. Let Your liberating power establish a peaceful environment in our home. In Jesus' name.

11. Father, I declare Your power over the challenges in my marriage. Break and release us from any hindrance to peace. In Jesus' name.

12. Lord, I trust in Your promises of tranquility. Infuse our marriage with Your peace that surpasses understanding. In Jesus' name.

13. Father, I stand against any external influence causing unrest in my marriage. Let Your divine intervention protect and restore peace. In Jesus' name.

14. Lord, I plead for Your mercy and peace. Fill our home with Your divine grace and serenity. In Jesus' name.

15. Heavenly Father, I surrender the conflicts and worries in my marriage to You. Let Your peace reign, bringing unity and joy to our home. In Jesus' name.

Chapter 19

Prayer For Promotion

Trust in the Lord with all your heart and lean not on your own understanding; in all your ways submit to him, and he will make your paths straight.

Proverbs 3:5-6 (NIV)

19.1. Prayer for Godly Promotion

1. Heavenly Father, I approach Your throne with gratitude, seeking Your divine hand for godly promotion in my life. In Jesus' name.

2. Lord, I acknowledge You as the source of all promotion. Open doors that no one can shut and elevate me according to Your will. In Jesus' name.

3. Father, I plead the blood of Jesus over my ambitions and endeavors. Let Your favor surround me and pave the way for godly promotion. In Jesus' name.

4. Lord, break down the barriers to promotion and success in my life. Let Your guidance and favor propel me forward. In Jesus' name.

5. Father, I stand on Your promises for promotion. Let Your divine influence position me for godly elevation. In Jesus' name.

6. Lord, I release humility and diligence in my pursuits. Let Your grace and wisdom be evident in every step toward godly promotion. In Jesus' name.

7. Father, I invite Your Spirit to guide my career and ambitions. Lead me in the path of godly promotion and success. In Jesus' name.

8. Lord, dismantle any obstacle or opposition hindering my godly promotion. Let Your wisdom guide me to overcome challenges. In Jesus' name.

9. Father, I rebuke every spirit of stagnation. Let Your divine intervention propel me into new levels of godly promotion. In Jesus' name.

10. Lord, break the chains of limitations in my life. Let Your liberating power establish a season of godly promotion. In Jesus' name.

11. Father, I declare Your power over every career challenge. Break and release me into the realm of godly promotion. In Jesus' name.

12. Lord, I trust in Your promises of elevation. Open doors that align with Your divine plan for my life. In Jesus' name.

13. Father, I stand against any form of injustice or unfair treatment in my pursuits. Let Your divine intervention secure my godly promotion. In Jesus' name.

14. Lord, I plead for Your mercy and favor. Uplift me in Your perfect timing and according to Your purpose. In Jesus' name.

15. Heavenly Father, I surrender my ambitions and desires for promotion to You. Let Your godly promotion be evident in my life, bringing glory to Your name. In Jesus' name.

19.2. Prayer to Claim Divine Blessings

1. Heavenly Father, I come before You with gratitude, seeking to claim the divine blessings You have in store for me. In Jesus' name.

2. Lord, I acknowledge You as the giver of every good and perfect gift. Open the floodgates of heaven and shower me with Your abundant blessings. In Jesus' name.

3. Father, I plead the blood of Jesus over my life, inviting Your blessings to flow in every area. Let Your favor surround me and manifest as divine blessings. In Jesus' name.

4. Lord, break down any barriers that may hinder Your blessings in my life. Let Your grace and favor bring forth a season of divine blessings. In Jesus' name.

5. Father, I stand on Your promises for abundance. Let Your divine influence pour blessings upon me and overflow into the lives of others. In Jesus' name.

6. Lord, I release gratitude and thanksgiving for past and future blessings. Let Your grace and mercy continue to manifest as divine blessings in my life. In Jesus' name.

7. Father, I invite Your Spirit to guide me in alignment with Your divine plan. Lead me to the path of divine blessings and prosperity. In Jesus' name.

8. Lord, dismantle any hindrance or opposition blocking the manifestation of Your blessings. Let Your wisdom guide me to receive Your divine favor. In Jesus' name.

9. Father, I rebuke every spirit of lack and insufficiency. Let Your divine intervention bring forth a bountiful season of blessings. In Jesus' name.

10. Lord, break the chains of scarcity and limitation. Let Your liberating power establish a continuous flow of divine blessings in my life. In Jesus' name.

11. Father, I declare Your power over every area of need. Break and release abundant blessings according to Your riches in glory. In Jesus' name.

12. Lord, I trust in Your promises of provision. Open doors of blessing and pour out Your divine abundance upon me. In Jesus' name.

13. Father, I stand against any form of lack or depletion. Let Your divine intervention secure a season of overflow and blessings. In Jesus' name.

14. Lord, I plead for Your mercy and favor. Shower me with Your divine blessings that I may be a channel of blessing to others. In Jesus' name.

15. Heavenly Father, I surrender my needs and desires to You. Let Your divine blessings flow in my life, bringing glory to Your name. In Jesus' name.

19.3. Prayer to Enter Your Inheritance

1. Heavenly Father, I approach Your throne with reverence, seeking to enter the inheritance You have prepared for me. In Jesus' name.

2. Lord, I acknowledge You as the giver of every good and perfect gift. Open the gates of my inheritance and lead me into the fullness of Your promises. In Jesus' name.

3. Father, I plead the blood of Jesus over my life, marking me as an heir to Your divine inheritance. Let Your favor and grace surround me. In Jesus' name.

4. Lord, break down any barriers that may hinder my entry into the inheritance You have ordained for me. Let Your guidance and favor pave the way. In Jesus' name.

5. Father, I stand on Your promises for abundance and prosperity. Let Your divine influence position me to receive the fullness of my inheritance. In Jesus' name.

6. Lord, I release faith and obedience in my journey towards inheritance. Let Your grace and wisdom be evident as I step into Your appointed blessings. In Jesus' name.

7. Father, I invite Your Spirit to lead me on the path of my divine inheritance. Guide me in alignment with Your perfect will. In Jesus' name.

8. Lord, dismantle any hindrance or opposition blocking my entrance into the inheritance. Let Your wisdom and favor guide me through every challenge. In Jesus' name.

9. Father, I rebuke every spirit of delay and denial. Let Your divine intervention accelerate my journey into the inheritance You have for me. In Jesus' name.

10. Lord, break the chains of fear and hesitation. Let Your liberating power establish my steps into the fullness of my inheritance. In Jesus' name.

11. Father, I declare Your power over every area of resistance. Break and release me into the richness of Your promises and inheritance. In Jesus' name.

12. Lord, I trust in Your promises of provision and prosperity. Open the doors of my inheritance and let Your abundance flow into my life. In Jesus' name.

13. Father, I stand against any form of spiritual opposition. Let Your divine intervention secure my entrance into the inheritance You have ordained. In Jesus' name.

14. Lord, I plead for Your mercy and favor. Guide me into my inheritance that I may walk in the fullness of Your purpose. In Jesus' name.

15. Heavenly Father, I surrender my journey into inheritance to You. Let Your divine guidance lead me into the richness of Your promises, bringing glory to Your name. In Jesus' name.

19.4. Prayer to Move from Poverty to Prosperity

1. Heavenly Father, I humbly come before Your throne, seeking Your divine intervention to move from poverty to prosperity. In Jesus' name.

2. Lord, I acknowledge You as the source of all wealth and abundance. Open the doors of prosperity and lead me into a season of financial breakthrough. In Jesus' name.

3. Father, I plead the blood of Jesus over my financial situation. Let Your favor and grace surround me, transforming my circumstances from poverty to prosperity. In Jesus' name.

4. Lord, break down any barriers that may be keeping me in a state of lack. Let Your guidance and favor pave the way for a journey from poverty to prosperity. In Jesus' name.

5. Father, I stand on Your promises for abundance. Let Your divine influence position me to receive the fullness of prosperity You have in store for me. In Jesus' name.

6. Lord, I release faith and diligence in my pursuit of prosperity. Let Your grace and wisdom be evident as I navigate the path from poverty to prosperity. In Jesus' name.

7. Father, I invite Your Spirit to lead me in alignment with Your financial plan. Guide me in making wise decisions that align with Your purpose for my life. In Jesus' name.

8. Lord, dismantle any hindrance or opposition blocking my financial breakthrough. Let Your wisdom and favor guide me through every financial challenge. In Jesus' name.

9. Father, I rebuke every spirit of financial lack and insufficiency. Let Your divine intervention accelerate my journey from poverty to prosperity. In Jesus' name.

10. Lord, break the chains of financial bondage. Let Your liberating power establish a continuous flow of prosperity into my life. In Jesus' name.

11. Father, I declare Your power over every area of financial struggle. Break and release me into the richness of Your promises for prosperity. In Jesus' name.

12. Lord, I trust in Your promises of provision and abundance. Open the doors of financial prosperity and let Your abundance flow into every aspect of my life. In Jesus' name.

13. Father, I stand against any form of financial oppression. Let Your divine intervention secure my journey from poverty to prosperity. In Jesus' name.

14. Lord, I plead for Your mercy and favor. Guide me on this journey, ensuring that my steps lead me into the prosperity You have ordained for me. In Jesus' name.

15. Heavenly Father, I surrender my financial situation to You. Let Your divine guidance lead me from poverty to prosperity, bringing glory to Your name. In Jesus' name.

19.5. Prayer for Divine Elevation

1. Heavenly Father, I bow before Your majesty, seeking Your divine intervention for elevation in every area of my life. In Jesus' name.

2. Lord, I acknowledge You as the lifter of my head and the source of all promotion. Open the doors of divine elevation and lift me to new heights. In Jesus' name.

3. Father, I plead the blood of Jesus over my journey toward elevation. Let Your favor and grace surround me, lifting me above every challenge. In Jesus' name.

4. Lord, break down any barriers that may hinder my elevation. Let Your guidance and favor pave the way for a season of divine promotion. In Jesus' name.

5. Father, I stand on Your promises for upliftment. Let Your divine influence position me to receive the fullness of elevation You have in store for me. In Jesus' name.

6. Lord, I release faith and obedience as I journey toward divine elevation. Let Your grace and wisdom be evident as I climb the steps of promotion. In Jesus' name.

7. Father, I invite Your Spirit to lead me in alignment with Your purpose for elevation. Guide me in making decisions that align with Your plan for my life. In Jesus' name.

8. Lord, dismantle any hindrance or opposition blocking my path to elevation. Let Your wisdom and favor guide me through every challenge. In Jesus' name.

9. Father, I rebuke every spirit of stagnation and limitation. Let Your divine intervention accelerate my journey toward divine elevation. In Jesus' name.

10. Lord, break the chains of mediocrity and small-mindedness. Let Your liberating power establish a continuous ascent toward divine elevation in my life. In Jesus' name.

11. Father, I declare Your power over every area of resistance to elevation. Break and release me into the fullness of the promotion You have planned for me. In Jesus' name.

12. Lord, I trust in Your promises of exaltation. Open the doors of divine elevation and let Your favor lift me to new levels of success. In Jesus' name.

13. Father, I stand against any form of setback or demotion. Let Your divine intervention secure my journey toward elevation. In Jesus' name.

14. Lord, I plead for Your mercy and favor. Guide me on this journey, ensuring that my steps lead me into the divine elevation You have ordained for me. In Jesus' name.

15. Heavenly Father, I surrender my life to Your divine plan for elevation. Let Your guidance lead me to new heights, bringing glory to Your name. In Jesus' name.

19.6. Prayer for Divine Breakthrough and Promotion

1. Father, I humbly seek Your breakthrough and promotion. In Jesus' name.

2. Lord, open doors for divine breakthrough and promotion. Lift me to new levels. In Jesus' name.

3. Father, I plead Jesus' blood for breakthrough. Surround me with favor and grace. In Jesus' name.

4. Lord, break barriers hindering my breakthrough. Guide me to divine promotion. In Jesus' name.

5. Father, I stand on Your promises. Let divine influence position me for fullness. In Jesus' name.

6. Lord, I release faith for divine breakthrough. Let grace and wisdom prevail. In Jesus' name.

7. Father, lead me in alignment with Your purpose. Guide decisions for breakthrough. In Jesus' name.

8. Lord, dismantle hindrances to my breakthrough. Let wisdom and favor prevail. In Jesus' name.

9. Father, rebuke stagnation. Accelerate my journey to breakthrough and promotion. In Jesus' name.

10. Lord, break chains of setbacks. Establish a continuous flow of promotion. In Jesus' name.

11. Father, declare power over resistance. Release me to fullness of promotion. In Jesus' name.

12. Lord, open doors of divine breakthrough. Let favor lift me to success. In Jesus' name.

13. Father, stand against setbacks. Secure my journey to breakthrough. In Jesus' name.

14. Lord, plead for mercy and favor. Guide me to ordained breakthrough. In Jesus' name.

15. Heavenly Father, surrendering to Your plan. Let guidance lead me to new heights. In Jesus' name.

19.7. Prayer to Overcome Satanic Oppositions

1. Heavenly Father, I bow before Your throne, acknowledging Your supremacy over all spiritual opposition. In Jesus' name.

2. Lord, I recognize the reality of spiritual warfare and the schemes of the enemy. Grant me the strength to overcome every satanic opposition. In Jesus' name.

3. Father, I plead the blood of Jesus over my life and declare victory over every satanic plot. Let Your divine protection shield me from the attacks of the enemy. In Jesus' name.

4. Lord, break down the strongholds of the enemy and nullify every satanic assignment against me. Let Your power prevail in the face of opposition. In Jesus' name.

5. Father, I stand on Your promises for victory over the enemy. Let Your divine influence position me to overcome every satanic opposition. In Jesus' name.

6. Lord, I release faith and courage as I confront the forces of darkness. Let Your grace and wisdom be evident as I navigate the challenges posed by satanic opposition. In Jesus' name.

7. Father, I invite Your Spirit to lead me in spiritual warfare. Guide me in discerning the tactics of the enemy and grant me the wisdom to counter every satanic plot. In Jesus' name.

8. Lord, dismantle any hindrance or opposition orchestrated by the evil one. Let Your wisdom and favor guide me through every spiritual battle. In Jesus' name.

9. Father, I rebuke every spirit of fear and intimidation from the enemy. Let Your divine intervention empower me to stand firm against satanic opposition. In Jesus' name.

10. Lord, break the chains of darkness that seek to bind and hinder my progress. Let Your liberating power establish a continuous victory over satanic opposition. In Jesus' name.

11. Father, I declare Your power over every demonic force aligned against me. Break and release me into the fullness of the victory You have secured. In Jesus' name.

12. Lord, I trust in Your promises of triumph. Open the doors of divine victory and let Your favor lead me to overcome every satanic opposition. In Jesus' name.

13. Father, I stand against any form of spiritual setback or defeat. Let Your divine intervention secure my victory over satanic opposition. In Jesus' name.

14. Lord, I plead for Your mercy and favor. Guide me in this spiritual battle, ensuring that my steps lead me to triumph over every satanic opposition. In Jesus' name.

15. Heavenly Father, I surrender my spiritual battles to Your authority. Let Your guidance and protection lead me to continuous victory, bringing glory to Your name. In Jesus' name.

19.8. Prayer to Meet Your Needs

1. Heavenly Father, I come before You with gratitude for Your promise to meet all my needs according to Your riches in glory. In Jesus' name.

2. Lord, You are my Provider, and I trust in Your faithfulness to supply every need. Open the windows of heaven and pour out Your blessings upon me. In Jesus' name.

3. Father, I bring before You my needs—physical, emotional, and spiritual. Let Your abundant provision flow into every area of my life. In Jesus' name.

4. Lord, I cast my anxieties upon You, knowing that You care for me. Provide for my daily necessities and grant me the wisdom to steward Your blessings well. In Jesus' name.

5. Father, I stand on Your Word that declares You are Jehovah Jireh, my Provider. Manifest Your provision in miraculous ways, exceeding my expectations. In Jesus' name.

6. Lord, I release faith for supernatural provision. Remove any obstacles hindering the fulfillment of my needs and let Your abundance overflow in my life. In Jesus' name.

7. Father, I invite Your Spirit to guide me in financial stewardship. Show me the path of wisdom in managing resources, and let Your prosperity abound. In Jesus' name.

8. Lord, break the chains of lack and insufficiency. Let Your generous hand meet my needs abundantly, demonstrating Your glory in my life. In Jesus' name.

9. Father, I rebuke every spirit of poverty and scarcity. Release Your provision to cover every area of lack and bring about a season of abundance. In Jesus' name.

10. Lord, I declare that my needs are met through Your unfailing love. Let Your provision be a testimony to Your goodness and faithfulness in my life. In Jesus' name.

11. Father, I trust in Your perfect timing. As I seek Your kingdom first, let all my needs be added unto me. Grant me patience and unwavering faith in Your provision. In Jesus' name.

12. Lord, I surrender my worries and concerns to You. Provide according to Your will, and let Your peace guard my heart as I trust in Your provision. In Jesus' name.

13. Father, I stand against any form of lack and scarcity. Let Your supernatural provision flow into every area of my life, bringing glory to Your name. In Jesus' name.

14. Lord, I plead for Your mercy and favor. Guide me in aligning my needs with Your purpose, and let Your provision bring about breakthroughs in my life. In Jesus' name.

15. Heavenly Father, I thank You in advance for meeting all my needs. Let Your provision be a testament to Your faithfulness and a source of gratitude in my heart. In Jesus' name.

19.9. Prayer for Divine Light to Manifest

1. Heavenly Father, I enter Your presence with a heart open to the manifestation of Your divine light. In Jesus' name.

2. Lord, be my source of radiant light, guiding every aspect of my life. Manifest Your divine brilliance. In Jesus' name.

3. Father, let Your divine light dispel darkness, revealing the path You set before me. Illuminate my journey. In Jesus' name.

4. Lord, Your light breaks shadows, unveiling hidden truths. Guide my steps with divine illumination. In Jesus' name.

5. Father, I release faith for Your light to manifest, exposing areas needing transformation. In Jesus' name.

6. Lord, I surrender to Your divine light, bringing revelation, wisdom, and discernment. Illuminate my understanding. In Jesus' name.

7. Father, Your light brings clarity to confusing situations. Manifest Your divine illumination in my life. In Jesus' name.

8. Lord, break spiritual darkness, bringing Your divine light to dispel confusion or doubt. In Jesus' name.

9. Father, rebuke spiritual blindness. Let Your divine light open my eyes to the beauty of Your ways. In Jesus' name.

10. Lord, Your light brings revelation and transformation. Manifest it in every area, guiding me in righteousness. In Jesus' name.

11. Father, I trust Your promise—Your Word is a lamp. Let divine light be my constant guide. In Jesus' name.

12. Lord, I surrender to Your light revealing hidden things. Expose and cleanse for clarity and understanding. In Jesus' name.

13. Father, stand against spiritual darkness. Let Your divine illumination prevail in every aspect of my life. In Jesus' name.

14. Lord, I plead for mercy and favor. Let Your divine light bring breakthroughs, revelation, and a deeper connection. In Jesus' name.

15. Heavenly Father, thank You for Your divine light. May it continue shining, leading me into a deeper relationship. In Jesus' name.

Chapter 20

Prayer Against Sexual Problems

Submit yourselves, then, to God. Resist the devil, and he will flee from you. Come near to God and he will come near to you. Wash your hands, you sinners, and purify your hearts, you double-minded.

James 4:7-8 (NIV)

20.1. Prayer to Annihilate Sexual Bondage

1. Lord, break the chains of sexual bondage in my life. In Jesus' name.

2. Father, cleanse my mind and heart from impure thoughts. In Jesus' name.

3. Lord, deliver me from the grip of lust and temptation. In Jesus' name.

4. Father, break every unholy soul tie. In Jesus' name.

5. Lord, heal the wounds causing sexual bondage. In Jesus' name.

6. Father, strengthen me to resist the lure of sin. In Jesus' name.

7. Lord, purify my desires and make them align with Your will. In Jesus' name.

8. Father, renew my mind with Your Word. In Jesus' name.

9. Lord, replace lust with love and purity. In Jesus' name.

10. Father, guard my eyes and heart from temptation. In Jesus' name.

11. Lord, grant me strength to flee from sexual immorality. In Jesus' name.

12. Father, release Your healing over past wounds. In Jesus' name.

13. Lord, break the chains of addiction. In Jesus' name.

14. Father, restore purity to my thoughts and actions. In Jesus' name.

15. Lord, fill me with Your Spirit, breaking every bond of sexual sin. In Jesus' name.

20.2. Prayer to Thwart Drunkenness

1. Lord, break the chains of drunkenness in my life. In Jesus' name.

2. Father, grant me the strength to resist the lure of alcohol. In Jesus' name.

3. Lord, heal the root causes leading to excessive drinking. In Jesus' name.

4. Father, renew my mind with Your Word, guiding me away from drunkenness. In Jesus' name.

5. Lord, replace the desire for alcohol with self-control. In Jesus' name.

6. Father, break every bond of addiction to alcohol. In Jesus' name.

7. Lord, fill me with Your Spirit, providing a way out from drunkenness. In Jesus' name.

8. Father, surround me with support for a sober lifestyle. In Jesus' name.

9. Lord, break the cycle of dependency on alcohol. In Jesus' name.

10. Father, cleanse my body and mind from the effects of alcohol. In Jesus' name.

11. Lord, grant me clarity to see the destructive nature of drunkenness. In Jesus' name.

12. Father, deliver me from the stronghold of alcoholism. In Jesus' name.

13. Lord, break the influence of peer pressure leading to drunkenness. In Jesus' name.

14. Father, fill me with Your love, satisfying the void that drives to drink. In Jesus' name.

15. Lord, empower me to choose sobriety over the allure of drunkenness. In Jesus' name.

20.3. Prayer to Eliminate Satanic Weakness

1. Lord, break the chains of satanic weakness in my life. In Jesus' name.

2. Father, strengthen me against every attack of the enemy. In Jesus' name.

3. Lord, fortify my spirit against satanic influences. In Jesus' name.

4. Father, empower me to resist every temptation from the evil one. In Jesus' name.

5. Lord, fill me with Your strength to overcome satanic weaknesses. In Jesus' name.

6. Father, break every satanic stronghold that weakens my faith. In Jesus' name.

7. Lord, shield me from the schemes of the enemy. In Jesus' name.

8. Father, release Your power to eliminate satanic vulnerabilities. In Jesus' name.

9. Lord, grant me discernment to recognize and reject satanic attacks. In Jesus' name.

10. Father, fortify my mind against the lies and deceptions of the enemy. In Jesus' name.

11. Lord, cover me with the armor of God to stand against satanic weakness. In Jesus' name.

12. Father, break the grip of spiritual lethargy and apathy. In Jesus' name.

13. Lord, strengthen my prayer life to overcome satanic assaults. In Jesus' name.

14. Father, empower me to walk in victory over every satanic weakness. In Jesus' name.

15. Lord, fill me with Your Spirit, dispelling every form of satanic weakness. In Jesus' name.

20.4. Prayer to Break the Yoke of Sexual Demons

1. Lord, break the yoke of sexual demons in my life. In Jesus' name.

2. Father, cleanse my mind and heart from impure influences. In Jesus' name.

3. Lord, deliver me from the grip of lustful thoughts and desires. In Jesus' name.

4. Father, break every unholy soul tie with sexual demons. In Jesus' name.

5. Lord, heal the wounds causing bondage to sexual demons. In Jesus' name.

6. Father, strengthen me to resist the lure of sexual temptation. In Jesus' name.

7. Lord, purify my desires and make them align with Your will. In Jesus' name.

8. Father, renew my mind with Your Word, breaking the yoke of sexual bondage. In Jesus' name.

9. Lord, replace lust with love and purity. In Jesus' name.

10. Father, guard my eyes and heart from the influence of sexual demons. In Jesus' name.

11. Lord, grant me strength to flee from sexual immorality and demonic influences. In Jesus' name.

12. Father, release Your healing over past wounds connected to sexual demons. In Jesus' name.

13. Lord, break the chains of addiction to sexual demons. In Jesus' name.

14. Father, restore purity to my thoughts and actions. In Jesus' name.

15. Lord, fill me with Your Spirit, breaking every yoke of sexual demons. In Jesus' name.

20.5. Prayer Against Jezebel Spirits

1. Lord, I rebuke and bind every Jezebel spirit operating in my life. In Jesus' name.

2. Father, expose and dismantle the schemes of Jezebel in my relationships. In Jesus' name.

3. Lord, break the influence of Jezebel spirits in my workplace and community. In Jesus' name.

4. Father, protect me from manipulation and control by Jezebel spirits. In Jesus' name.

5. Lord, reveal the tactics of Jezebel and grant me discernment. In Jesus' name.

6. Father, shield my mind and heart from the attacks of Jezebel. In Jesus' name.

7. Lord, break the power of seduction and manipulation by Jezebel. In Jesus' name.

8. Father, release Your fire to consume every spirit of witchcraft and Jezebel. In Jesus' name.

9. Lord, strengthen me to resist the allure of Jezebel spirits. In Jesus' name.

10. Father, expose the hidden works of Jezebel in my life and surroundings. In Jesus' name.

11. Lord, break every unholy alliance with Jezebelic influences. In Jesus' name.

12. Father, grant me the courage to confront and overcome Jezebel spirits. In Jesus' name.

13. Lord, purify my relationships from Jezebelic manipulations. In Jesus' name.

14. Father, cut off the supply lines of Jezebel spirits in my life. In Jesus' name.

15. Lord, fill me with Your Spirit, breaking the influence of Jezebel once and for all. In Jesus' name.

20.6. Prayer for Victory Over Immorality

1. Lord, grant me victory over the chains of immorality. In Jesus' name.

2. Father, cleanse my heart and mind from impure thoughts. In Jesus' name.

3. Lord, deliver me from the grip of immoral desires and temptations. In Jesus' name.

4. Father, break every unholy soul tie connected to immorality. In Jesus' name.

5. Lord, heal the wounds causing bondage to immoral influences. In Jesus' name.

6. Father, strengthen me to resist the allure of immoral behaviors. In Jesus' name.

7. Lord, purify my desires and make them align with Your will. In Jesus' name.

8. Father, renew my mind with Your Word, breaking the chains of immorality. In Jesus' name.

9. Lord, replace lust with love and purity. In Jesus' name.

10. Father, guard my eyes and heart from the influence of immorality. In Jesus' name.

11. Lord, grant me strength to flee from immoral actions and influences. In Jesus' name.

12. Father, release Your healing over past wounds connected to immorality. In Jesus' name.

13. Lord, break the chains of addiction to immoral behaviors. In Jesus' name.

14. Father, restore purity to my thoughts and actions. In Jesus' name.

15. Lord, fill me with Your Spirit, breaking every yoke of immorality. In Jesus' name.

Chapter 21

Prayer Against Household Wickedness

For our struggle is not against flesh and blood, but against the rulers, against the authorities, against the powers of this dark world and against the spiritual forces of evil in the heavenly realms.

Ephesians 6:12 (NIV)

21.1. Prayer to Live Above Fear

1. Lord, banish fear from my heart, replacing it with Your perfect love. In Jesus' name.

2. Father, fortify my spirit to live fearlessly in Your strength. In Jesus' name.

3. Lord, break the chains of anxiety, granting me peace that surpasses all understanding. In Jesus' name.

4. Father, fill me with courage to face every challenge without fear. In Jesus' name.

5. Lord, I declare freedom from fear, trusting in Your unfailing promises. In Jesus' name.

6. Father, dispel fear and empower me to walk in boldness and faith. In Jesus' name.

7. Lord, I reject the spirit of fear; instead, I embrace Your spirit of power and sound mind. In Jesus' name.

8. Father, shield me from fear's grip, allowing me to live victoriously. In Jesus' name.

9. Lord, release Your peace that transcends fear in every aspect of my life. In Jesus' name.

10. Father, I break the power of fear over my mind and heart. In Jesus' name.

11. Lord, grant me confidence in Your sovereignty, dispelling all fears. In Jesus' name.

12. Father, empower me to confront fears with unwavering faith. In Jesus' name.

13. Lord, I declare freedom from the bondage of fear. In Jesus' name.

14. Father, fill me with Your love, casting out all fear. In Jesus' name.

15. Lord, I choose faith over fear, knowing You are with me. In Jesus' name.

21.2. Prayer to Eliminate Satanic Fear

1. Lord, break the grip of satanic fear over my life. In Jesus' name.

2. Father, release Your light to dispel the darkness of satanic fear. In Jesus' name.

3. Lord, I reject the spirit of satanic fear, embracing Your spirit of power and courage. In Jesus' name.

4. Father, dismantle every stronghold of satanic fear in my thoughts and heart. In Jesus' name.

5. Lord, I declare victory over satanic fear through the power of Your Word. In Jesus' name.

6. Father, fill me with Your presence, casting out all satanic fear. In Jesus' name.

7. Lord, I break the chains of satanic fear, trusting in Your sovereignty. In Jesus' name.

8. Father, empower me to stand firm against the attacks of satanic fear. In Jesus' name.

9. Lord, release Your angels to guard me against satanic fear. In Jesus' name.

10. Father, I declare freedom from the torment of satanic fear. In Jesus' name.

11. Lord, cover me with the blood of Jesus, rendering satanic fear powerless. In Jesus' name.

12. Father, I rebuke every spirit of darkness causing satanic fear. In Jesus' name.

13. Lord, let Your perfect love cast out all traces of satanic fear. In Jesus' name.

14. Father, I choose faith over satanic fear, knowing You are my refuge. In Jesus' name.

15. Lord, I declare peace in the midst of satanic fear, for You are my stronghold. In Jesus' name.

21.3. Prayer Against Household Attacks

1. Lord, I secure my home with Your protective hedge. In Jesus' name.

2. Father, shield my family from all forms of spiritual attacks. In Jesus' name.

3. Lord, I rebuke every evil force attempting to infiltrate my household. In Jesus' name.

4. Father, surround my home with Your angels to repel any attacks. In Jesus' name.

5. Lord, I declare the blood of Jesus over every member of my household. In Jesus' name.

6. Father, fortify the walls of my home against spiritual intruders. In Jesus' name.

7. Lord, break the influence of every negative force in my household. In Jesus' name.

8. Father, I bind and cast out any demonic presence in my home. In Jesus' name.

9. Lord, cover my family with the armor of God to withstand attacks. In Jesus' name.

10. Father, I proclaim peace and unity within my household. In Jesus' name.

11. Lord, let Your light dispel any darkness seeking to harm my family. In Jesus' name.

12. Father, establish Your divine order and protection in my household. In Jesus' name.

13. Lord, I reject any form of spiritual oppression within my home. In Jesus' name.

14. Father, release Your fire to consume every negative influence. In Jesus' name.

15. Lord, I stand firm in faith, trusting Your protection over my household. In Jesus' name.

21.4. Prayer for Redemption From the Redeemer

1. Lord Jesus, I come before You, seeking redemption for my soul. In Jesus' name.

2. Savior, cleanse me with Your precious blood and redeem my life. In Jesus' name.

3. Redeemer, break the chains of sin that bind me. In Jesus' name.

4. Lord, I surrender my past, present, and future to Your redeeming grace. In Jesus' name.

5. Jesus, redeem every broken area of my life and restore me. In Jesus' name.

6. Savior, I receive Your redemption that brings forgiveness and healing. In Jesus' name.

7. Redeemer, lift me from the pit of despair and set my feet on solid ground. In Jesus' name.

8. Lord, I declare Your redemption over every aspect of my being. In Jesus' name.

9. Jesus, redeem my mind, heart, and spirit from all bondage. In Jesus' name.

10. Savior, I embrace the freedom and redemption You offer. In Jesus' name.

11. Redeemer, let Your mercy and grace redeem my mistakes and failures. In Jesus' name.

12. Lord, I thank You for the power of Your redeeming love in my life. In Jesus' name.

13. Jesus, break the chains of guilt and shame with Your redeeming love. In Jesus' name.

14. Redeemer, transform my brokenness into a testimony of Your redeeming power. In Jesus' name.

15. Lord, I stand in gratitude for Your continuous redemption in my journey. In Jesus' name.

21.5. Prayer to Overpower Household Wickedness

1. Lord, expose and dismantle every form of wickedness in my household. In Jesus' name.

2. Father, let Your light shine and dispel the darkness of household wickedness. In Jesus' name.

3. Lord, break the power of every evil influence operating in my home. In Jesus' name.

4. Father, I rebuke and cast out every spirit of wickedness in my household. In Jesus' name.

5. Lord, cover my family with Your protective shield against household wickedness. In Jesus' name.

6. Father, release Your angels to guard and protect my home from wicked schemes. In Jesus' name.

7. Lord, let the fire of Your Holy Spirit consume every form of household wickedness. In Jesus' name.

8. Father, I stand on Your promises to resist and overpower any form of evil in my household. In Jesus' name.

9. Lord, I declare peace, love, and unity, displacing all wickedness from my home. In Jesus' name.

10. Father, break every generational curse and pattern of wickedness in my family. In Jesus' name.

11. Lord, empower me to stand firm against the wiles of household wickedness. In Jesus' name.

12. Father, I plead the blood of Jesus over every member of my household for protection. In Jesus' name.

13. Lord, let the presence of the Holy Spirit be a barrier against all forms of wickedness. In Jesus' name.

14. Father, grant wisdom and discernment to identify and overcome household wickedness. In Jesus' name.

15. Lord, establish Your divine order in my home, eradicating all traces of household wickedness. In Jesus' name.

Remain Blessed!

Made in United States
Troutdale, OR
01/12/2024

16908899R00146